PORTUGAL
1001 Sights

An Archaeological and Historical Guide

PORTUGAL
1001 Sights

An Archaeological and Historical Guide

James M. Anderson
and
M. Sheridan Lea

UNIVERSITY OF CALGARY PRESS
ROBERT HALE • LONDON

University of Calgary Press
2500 University Drive N.W.
Calgary, Alberta, Canada T2N 1N4

Robert Hale Limited
Clerkenwell House
Clerkenwell Green
London ECIR OHT

Canadian Cataloguing in Publication Data
Anderson, James M. (James Maxwell), 1933-
  Portugal, 1001 sights

  Includes bibliographical references and index.
  ISBN 1-895176-41-7 (University of Calgary Press)
  ISBN 0-7090-5606-0 (Robert Hale Limited)

  1. Portugal—Guidebooks. 2. Portugal—Antiquities—
Guidebooks. 3. Excavations (Archaeology)—Portugal—
Guidebooks. 4. Portugal—History. I. Lea, M. Sheridan,
1932- II. Title.
DP516.A52 1994   914.6904'44   C94-910605-4

COMMITTED TO THE DEVELOPMENT OF CULTURE AND THE ARTS

Printed and bound in Canada by DW Friesen.

♾ This book is printed on acid-free paper.

For the people of Portugal
and especially
the dedicated archaeologists
without whom this book
would not have been possible.

CONTENTS

ACKNOWLEDGEMENTS

The authors gratefully acknowledge assistance given in Portugal by:

Dr. Theodor Hauschild and Dra. Philine Kalb of the German Archaeological Institute, Lisboa.

Dr. Fernando Campos de Sousa Real, Director, Departamento de Arqueologia, IPPC, Lisboa.

Dr. António Cardim Ribeiro and Dra. Teresa Simões Paula, Museu de Sintra.

Dr. António Carlos Silva, Director, Divisão de Arqueologia, Direcção Regional de Évora.

Dra. Maria Clara Farinha, Deputy Director, International Department, Fundação Calouste Gulbenkian, Lisboa.

Dr. Michael Kunst, Museu de Torres Vedras.

Dr. F. Nunes Ribeiro, Beja.

Dr. Joaquim Figueira Mestre and Sr. José Luiz Soares of the Biblioteca Municipal, Beja.

Dr. João Luís Cardoso and Dra. Conceição Serra of Centro do Estudos Arqueólogicos Serviços Técnicos da Câmara Municipal, Oeiras.

Dr. João Carlos Lopes, Director, Biblioteca e Museu Municipal de Torres Novas.

Dra. Salete da Ponte, Tomar.

Sra. Judith Peixoto of the Canadian Embassy, Lisboa.

Prof. Nuno de Norinha Mendoça, Universidade de Évora.

Dr. Manuel Albino Penteado Neiva, Dr. Rui Manuel Carvalheiro da Cunha and Sra. Ana Cristina Lemos Ferreira of the Câmara Municipal, Esposende.

Sr. António Pita of ADT/NA, Castelo de Vide (Portalegre).

José Mota Alves, Vereador da Educação, Câmara Municipal, Vila Verde.

Sra. Ana de Almeida Alves de Oliveira of Galego Santa María.

Sr. António Augusto de Carvalho and Sra. María Angélica de Lima Teixeira of Carrazeda de Ansiães.

Sr. José Braga, Museu de Arqueologia, Serpa.

Sr./Sra Eduardo Correia Arsénio, Vilamoura.

Armando Martins Torres Nunes, Sintra.

Mario Nunes, Câmara Municipal de Oeiras.

Sra. María Veríssimo Lopes Pereira of Mazouco.

Umberto Santos Castelo, Marisa Andreia Gregorio Fialho, Susana Maria Gregorio Claudio of Vale de Telhas.

Paulo Sergio Salgueiro of Carlão, Paulo Sergio Jesus Sousa, Manuel Fernando Ferreira da Silva Fernandes, Hernâni Mateus Lima da Silva of Bagunte.

Sr. Jorge de Carvalho Furtado and Sra. Maria da Conceição Soeiro de Carvalho Furtado.

The Guarda Nacional Republicana (GNR) of Almendra.

We should also like to thank the following for their help and encouragement in the preparation of this book: Siwan and Corri, Virginia and Max Anderson, Shirley and Bob Anderson, Mary Ayton, Wyn Boxall, Jack Bruce, David Corre, Eileen Christopherson, Audrey and Bob Cuthbertson, Doris and Jim Dempster,

Beth Evans, Margaret and Richard Evans, Lisa Hamilton, Dr. Risto and Mrs. Rosemary Härmä, Françoise and Lucien Labedade, Rudolph Langen, Maribel and Fernando López, Munroe MacPhee, Moira and Sandy McRobbie, Sr. and Sra. Piero Porcari, Dr. Carol Prager, Dr. Joel Prager, Verna and Bryan Pryce,Michel Queyrane, June and Jeremy Ryan-Bell, Elaine Sorensen, Dr. Tim and Mrs. Heather Travers, Dr. Jürgen and Mrs. Bertha Untermann, Adrienne and Rex Wilkinson.

Thanks go also to Ford Graphics of Fordingbridge, England, and in particular to Paul Killinger who gave a great deal of time and help toward the production of this book.

We are grateful for the hospitality consistently offered to us by Anne and Gordon Anderson, Nancy and Len Bowley, Jill and Paul Killinger, and Jean and Marie-Alice Larroque.

The authors also wish to express their gratitude to The University of Calgary Press and especially to Shirley Onn, Director, John King, Production Editor, Cliff Kadatz, Marta Styk and Joan Barton.

The authors would like to thank IMS Aços Especiais, Lda. and its Director Geral in Portugal, Sr. Jorge de Carvalho Furtado, whose generous financial assistance helped make possible the publication of this book.

MAPS

PREFACE

Of the thousands of sites found in mainland Portugal, some are well-preserved, some are neglected and continuing their long process of decay while others have degenerated into heaps of rubble or disappeared altogether. The degree of protection and preservation of ancient monuments is always proportional to the money available and Portugal has never been a wealthy country. Many pressing future needs take priority over the past.

In the more remote areas of the country, removed from modern development, historic sites, even those unprotected, have often weathered the ravages of time diminished only by souvenir collectors and some re-utilization of the stone by local residents. In other regions, especially those which have undergone concentrated tourist growth or intensive agricultural pursuits such as the southern Algarvian coast, the once numerous ancient sites have often been totally obliterated. Similarly, the unremitting expansion of major cities and their surroundings, such as Lisboa, has effectively effaced countless relics of past civilizations. Of catastrophic consequence for irreplaceable ancient art has been the construction of dams and the resultant flooding of rupestrian paintings and engravings in the interior of the country.

In spite of the economic exigencies of the nation which have often been detrimental and even fatal to the preservation of its historical record, there are still many thought-provoking ancient sites that amply reward the inquisitive visitor. Indeed, for such a small country, Portugal is still most generous in archaeological interests.

It is of course true that, like historical monuments everywhere, from lowly graves to noble temples, those in Portugal have been looted, vandalized and destroyed practically from the time of their inception. The Romans, for example, robbed the accessible tombs of their predecessors, the barbarian tribes destroyed Roman monuments, Moslems at times sacked Christian churches and reconquering Christians rent asunder Moslem mosques in zealous programs of rebuilding them as churches or destroying all traces of the infidel. Only those structures hidden from view under intentional mounds of earth such as graves, or hidden in the course of time by windblown sands have escaped the ravages of treasure-hunters both ancient and modern. Useful structures such as bridges and roads, if not in the way of 'progress', have been spared destruction.

While the past has not been kind to the relics of bygone civilizations, the present seems to offer more hope of preserving what is left. Modern construction must stop while newly uncovered sites are examined and, if found worthy, protected. No longer are churches and houses being built with the stones quarried from a Roman villa. No longer are precious Roman mosaics ripped from the ground and carried off as souvenirs. The Portuguese are becoming more aware and concerned about their birthright and the story the ancient stones have to tell about their past.

Pride in their heritage was brought home to the authors even in the small villages such as Vale de Telhas (Bragança) where practically the entire population turned out upon our arrival and led us around in a solemn procession while enthusiastic youngsters pointed out every conceivable stone that could have some link with the remote past. We were the cause of more than one child returning late to school that afternoon.

It is the purpose of this book to assist the traveller, the visitor to Portugal, with the location, condition and evaluation of archaeological sites and to place these within a meaningful historical perspective. Specific directions are given to the more interesting places since many are inadequately signposted, if at all. Many sites, for example, a Roman city, have several sights and these are generally enumerated to help determine beforehand what is there. Adequate maps are given of the areas in question. At major locations, site plans may be obtained at the entrance. However, it is not necessary to travel to Portugal to appreciate its past and to enjoy the story contained in the following pages.

This volume portrays the history of Portugal from the earliest times down to nearly the end of the Moslem conquest and the birth of the kingdom in the twelfth century A.D. although the country's current boundaries were not fully established until the thirteenth century. An exception is made in the case of the Jewish communities which existed until the sixteenth century as a unique and enduring influence.

This book can never be complete since new sites are discovered every year when the soil is disturbed by new construction projects and as known sites, now under the ground, are excavated. There are also many on-going excavations with new details to report. At the same time, some excavated sites are re-covered to protect them from the elements and from treasure hunters. At one site when the authors visited the on-going excavation of a dolmen, the archaeologist in charge asked us not to report the location of the dig for fear the place would become the target of nocturnal operations by artifact seekers.

Nor can this book be a definitive statement of specific directions since Portugal continues to be engaged in massive road building and autoroutes are making the old road network obsolete.

Certainly the wonder and admiration of ancient builders, the architecture of sublime imagination depicted in their great tombs, temples, and towns, can never become obsolete.

INTRODUCTION

The historical sites and sights described in this book cover primarily the period from the first appearance of man on the western fringes of the Iberian peninsula to the emergence of the kingdom of Portugal. While it is true that there is much to see and enjoy in Portugal which corresponds to periods after this time, this has been adequately described in other guidebooks to the country.

Much of the information concerning the earlier periods is, at best, sketchy, conjectural and often polemical but the physical remains of Medieval, ancient and prehistoric cultures may still be viewed in situ in some places and it is to these the reader's attention is mainly directed. Here, at these sometimes forgotten and neglected places, one may enjoy the solitude while pondering relics of times long past.

If they have not fallen into private hands, artifacts have been removed from most sites to museums and the traveller may wish to repair to these in order to become more familiar with certain aspects of a site or historical epoch. Museums, many with good archaeological collections, are found in all major cities and many of the smaller towns. Some sites have museums in situ.

Cultural phases in the historical record of human undertaking reached different areas of the globe at widely differing times, a fact the reader may wish to take into account while examining the early cultural evolution of Portugal. For example, the smelting of iron and its use in weapons and ornaments, known to the Hittites in Anatolia about the middle of the second millennium B.C., was first introduced by Celtic people to the Bronze Age tribes of ancient Portugal nearly a thousand years later. Ironworking techniques did not begin in the Americas until the coming of the Europeans about two thousand years after that.

Traces of man in Portugal date back to Paleolithic times but there is now little to see in Paleolithic occupation sites, caves, grottos and open-air camps. As the Paleolithic period came to a close on the Iberian peninsula, settled Neolithic communities were already established in southwest Asia as early as nine thousand B.C. employing techniques of animal domestication, crop raising, pottery and specialized crafts. Neolithic cultural features became established in Portugal sometime in the fifth millennium B.C. Settled Neolithic cultures have bequeathed enduring stone structures in the form of megaliths or dolmens and other types of burial chambers. The earliest of the dolmens, however, predate the great sepulchre tombs (pyramids) of Egypt by over a thousand years.

Bronze metallurgy for implements and weapons appears to have been introduced onto the Atlantic fringes of the Iberian peninsula from the Bronze Age settlement of El Argar, in the province of Almería, in Spain, sometime around the middle of the second millennium B.C. but the use of the metal dates back a millennium before in the Near East and Eastern Mediterranean.

Celtic tribes appear to have arrived on the Atlantic seaboard near the beginning of the first millennium B.C. and many of their walled, mountaintop, stone villages called castros, sometimes taken over from earlier inhabitants, are still there to behold. These ancient peoples guarded their flocks, cultivated small patches of vegetables and cereals, warred with one another and worshipped natural objects far from the mainstream of world history.

While the preliterate Celts were constructing their remote hilltop villages of ancient Lusitania, Greek cities such as Athens and Sparta had already reached a high degree of civilization aided by the use of writing. In the first half of the first millennium B.C., Phoenicians and a little later Greeks came to the Atlantic littoral to establish trading stations and exploit the mineral and marine wealth of the region. They found already advanced peoples: the Conii and Turdetani in the south. Untouched by these developments the northern Celtic inhabitants of the country remained secluded in their isolated villages.

All eventually gave way to massive Roman influence won by the sword and as part of the Roman empire, the territory that would become the modern state of Portugal adopted the Latin language and customs. Roman cities and towns make up the most impressive ruins of that ancient period but the conquerors paid a heavy price to subdue the intractable Celtic tribes. Germanic and other eastern peoples, generally referred to as barbarians, administered the *coup de grâce* to the flagging Roman empire in this part of the world as elsewhere, but they left little to show for their sojourn in ancient Lusitania. They decimated themselves by their own internal struggles. The remaining *force majeur*, the Visigoths, faded rapidly from history as a result of the Moslem invasion in the year 711 which swept across the Hispanic peninsula.

Slowly and tentatively Christian forces over the next centuries reclaimed the land, culminating, along the Atlantic coasts of the Iberian peninsula, in the kingdom of Portugal. During those violent and unsettled times one could hardly have guessed that little Portugal would rise to the lofty pinnacle of world prestige as the foremost nation of maritime explorers.

Geography

Situated in southwest Europe on the western side of the Iberian peninsula, the Republic of Portugal covers an area of 88,550 square kilometres. The capital city is Lisboa. The Portuguese islands of Madeira and the Azores, fifteenth century discoveries in the Atlantic ocean, are not included in this treatment of historical sites.

Occupying about one-fifth of the Iberian peninsula, the country is bordered by Spain on the east and north along a 1,215-kilometre frontier. The Atlantic Ocean, on the west and south, comprises the coastal strip of Portugal and is 848 kilometres long but with only a few good harbours. Only 218 kilometres from east to west at the widest point, the country is 561 kilometres from north to south.

The modern boundaries are somewhat different from those of antiquity when the Roman administrative divisions applied. For example, during the time of the Roman Empire, much of the country belonged to the province of Lusitania with its capital at present-day Mérida in Spain. Then, Lusitania was bounded in the north by the river Douro and the land beyond was in the province of Tarraconensis.

The present geographical boundaries of mainland Portugal, following Christian advances southward, were consolidated by Afonso III in 1249 with the conquest from the Moslems of the southernmost region, the Algarve.

There are pronounced variations in Portuguese terrain and climate which have always had an effect on human settlement patterns, and since early times, the bountiful sea and river valleys have attracted fishermen and shellfish gatherers. The limestone caves of the coastal areas offered shelter to prehistoric peoples, and the hills and mountains of the north, protected by natural ramparts, were suitable for hilltop villages. The open plains of the south offered agricultural prospects for later, more domestic, civilizations.

The major rivers (from north to south)—the Minho, Lima, Douro, Vouga, Mondego, Tejo, Sado and Mira—all flow in a westerly direction into the Atlantic Ocean while the Guadiana flows southward, some of it along the Portuguese-Spanish border.

The temperate northern coastal strip of the Iberian Peninsula with bountiful rainfall and natural forest cover (oak, elm, ash) extends down the western seaboard as far as the Tejo estuary.

Mainland Portugal is divisible into eleven historical provinces which more-or-less define the natural regions of the country. These in turn have been subdivided into eighteen administrative districts named by their corresponding capital cities. (See map 5, p. 34.)

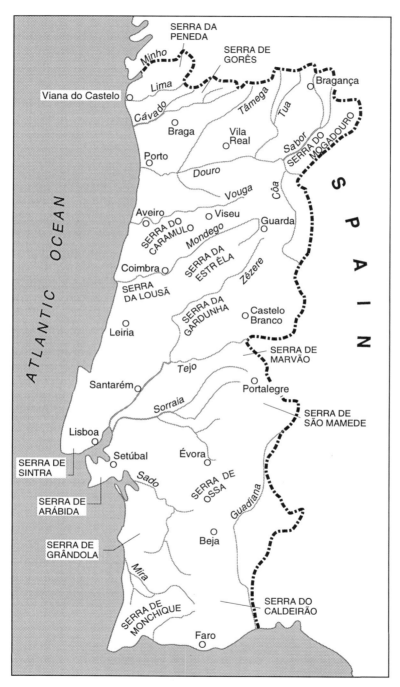

Map 1. Physical features of Portugal

The North

The northwest region of the Minho, districts of Viana do Castelo and Braga, consists of a jumble of granite hills covered by dense forests with the exception of the Gerês and Peneda mountains in the east along the Galician border with their exposed rocky summits. Further inland, to the east, the landlocked region of Tras-os-Montes ("behind the mountains"), containing the districts of Bragança and Vila Real, is watered by the rivers Tâmega, Tua and Sabor, all flowing southward into the Douro. In Bragança the land rises to an exposed, remote and once isolated highland lacerated by deep valleys and with a vigorous upland continental climate.

Further south, the Douro river, a continuation of the Spanish Duero, wends its way through the hills of Douro Litoral to Porto and the sea. In Beira Litoral (Beira "border, edge") where much of the land is low lying marshes and sand dunes along the Atlantic shores, the hills again rise toward the east culminating in Beira Alta and the lofty peaks of the Serra da Estrêla, the highest mountain range in the country. These mountains give rise to the Mondego river (and some of its tributaries) which passes through Coimbra on its way to the sea at Figueira da Foz, and to the southwest-flowing Zêzere, a major tributary of the river Tejo. South of the mountains, in Beira Baixa, the land begins to flatten out onto broad plains.

Estremadura, once the extremity of the Christian domains in the struggle with the Moslems, is essentially a land of undulating hills and fertile soil interrupted by the jagged outcroppings of the Sintra mountains and further south, across the Tejo, the Arrábida mountains. Inland the Ribatejo ("banks of the Tejo"), straddles the lower Tejo valley, much of it a broad alluvial plain. The river, a continuation of the Spanish Tajo flowing from the northeast to the southwest with its many tributaries, is the principal river of the country. Often cited by its Latin name Tagus, it enters the sea at the port of Lisboa.

The South

The portion of the country comprising the Alentejo, (old spelling Alemtejo) literally "beyond the Tejo," is primarily a land of rolling, open plains with the exception of a few ridges of mountains such as the Serra de São Mamede in the northeast and the Serra de Ossa east of Évora. It includes both the Alto "upper" and the Baixo "lower" Alentejo extending from the river Tejo to the Algarvian mountains. The climate is hot and dry in the summer and cool and wet in the winter. The olive, cork and holm oaks are the typical trees found here and there in small clusters but the area is known as O celeiro de Portugal or "the granary of Portugal." The region is drained primarily by the Guadiana River and tributaries of the River Sado.

The Alentejo is separated from the southernmost province of the Algarve by a line of hills in the west known as the Serra de Monchique and in the east by the Serra do Caldeirão. The Algarve consists of a relatively flat coastal strip across the bottom of the country. With a suave Mediterranean climate and fertile soil, the south coast is conducive to such crops as sugar, rice, and citrus fruits among others.

Portuguese towns pertain to freguesias (parishes), concelhos (municipalities) and districts. For example, the concelho of Alijó belongs to the district of Vila Real and has about twenty-five thousand inhabitants spread throughout nineteen freguesias containing forty-nine towns or villages.

For a detailed examination of Portuguese geography, climate, vegetation, and geology, see D. Stanislawski, *The Individuality of Portugal* (Austin, 1959).

PART ONE
HISTORICAL BACKGROUND

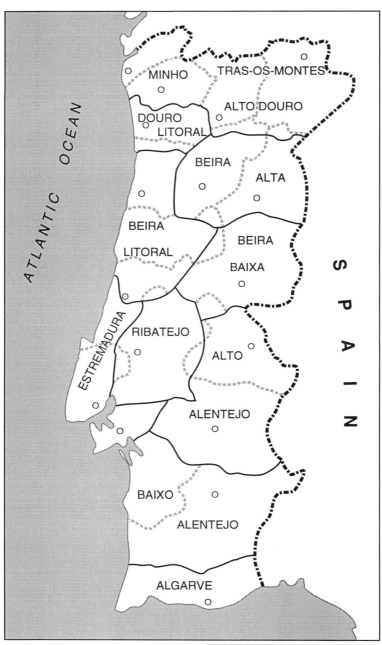

Map 2. Old provinces of Portugal

———	Old provinces
∗∗∗∗∗∗∗	Boundaries of districts
○	District capitals

1. Paleolithic Period

Lower Paleolithic

Homo erectus, contemporary with an early Pleistocene glaciation of about 550,000 years ago, has left traces of his existence in Portugal in the form of pebble tools designed for cutting and scraping. These are the earliest and most primitive of recognizable human artifacts—the oldest examples dating back over two million years in some parts of the world. They are produced by striking flakes from a stone to make a working edge. Such tools eventually developed into hand axes and choppers.

These Lower Paleolithic implements (*paleo* "old" + *lithic* "stone") have been found widely distributed throughout the country, particularly along the Atlantic seaboard at Vila Nova de Milfontes in the Alentejo, in Estremadura (where many of the limestone caves sheltered Paleolithic man), at Alpiarça in Santarém, in Leiria, and north of the Douro in the Minho area.

During an early interglacial period (about 450,000 years ago), the oceans rose to levels higher than today and many of the beaches in Portugal on which early man lived are now well out of reach of the sea.

The valley of the Tejo river has been a particularly fertile area for the study of primordial cultures: for example, a recent study of an Old Stone Age site near Vila Velha de Ródão, Castelo Branco, has revealed stone tools and the remains of large animals used for food such as horses, stags and elephants. The early Stone Age migrants may have crossed onto the Iberian peninsula from northwest Africa via the Straits of Gibraltar.

Middle Paleolithic

Middle Paleolithic artifacts, from ca. 100,000 to 35,000 thousand years ago, somewhat more refined than those of the previous period, have also been found in a variety of places throughout the country including caves, rock shelters and open- air sites. Again, river valleys such as the Tejo or the Sado, with their ancient alluvial terraces left behind by the river, have proven suitable places to look for the remains of these early societies. The tools of this stage were made from flaking off the core in a more precise operation than before. Flint flakes were chipped off to desired shape and size. The period is associated with Neanderthal man.

The grotto of Nova da Columbeira in the parish of Bombarral, a little north of Torres Vedras, is a good example of a Stone Age site. Discovered accidentally in the 1970s, some twenty levels of occupation have been excavated. The first eight have been associated with the Upper Paleolithic and the remainder with older periods. Besides stone tools such as scrapers and the bones of bear, hyena, leopard, wolf, and horse, there were also remains of the rhinoceros. A small human tooth, attributed to *Homo sapiens neanderthalensis*, or Neanderthal man, if correctly assessed, constitutes the oldest human fossil found in the country.

Upper Paleolithic

Unique in Portugal are the Upper Paleolithic cave paintings and engravings at Escoural in the district of Évora of ca. 35,000–10,000 years ago, a period of time that coincides with the appearance in the area of modern *Homo sapiens* who improved the flint tools of earlier societies and learned how to make better implements of bone, antler, wood and shell. They were responsible for the cave art throughout southwestern Europe.

The Upper Paleolithic is represented by sites scattered around the country. Many are open-air sites but grottos and caves continued to be occupied. Attributed to the Upper Paleolithic are rupestrian engravings of three animals in the open-air site near the village of Mazouco on the river Douro near the Spanish border, and several anthropomorphic statuettes discovered just inside the grotto of Toca do Pai Lopes near Setúbal. From the grotto of Caldeirão near Tomar came a stone incised on two sides with what could be representations of an animal and a person.

The majority of prominent Paleolithic sites so far found in Portugal are in the areas of Estremadura, Leiria and along the Tejo river valley. The Tejo river system was the lifeline of Paleolithic man and also of later peoples who settled along it and whose remains still exist in some places. Nowhere is this more clear than along its middle course (Médio Tejo) for a stretch of about fifty kilometres up to the Spanish border and for several kilometres of its tributaries, the Ocresa and the Pracana, where many rupestrian paintings were discovered. Unfortunately, this natural museum of European prehistoric art is today nearly all under the flood waters of local dams.

The valley of the lower Tejo (Baixo Tejo), especially in the area of Alpiarça where numerous pebble tools have been found in situ, attests to a long period of occupation by Paleolithic peoples.

For the visitor, however, there is generally nothing to see at these places except, at best, a grotto or cave where artifacts and animal bones were once found, but which are now in museums.

2. Mesolithic Period

The transition between the Paleolithic and Neolithic cultures is called Mesolithic (Greek *meso* "middle"). During this period there was a global climatic change and in Europe, as the last ice sheets from the period of the Würm glaciation covering large tracts of the continent gradually retreated, temperatures rose. Climatic changes and, probably, the effects of a growing population demanding more food, may have been alleviated by the gathering of crustaceans along the seashores and by fishing. Mesolithic man mastered the use of boats, nets and the fishhook.

Artifacts from this period have been discovered in several places in the country with the largest concentrations along river banks such as those of the Sado and the Muge—the latter a tributary of the Tejo near its mouth. Other sites are found along the Atlantic littoral from the Alentejo to Estremadura and further north as well as inland. Characteristic of Mesolithic habitation in Portugal are the shellmiddens (concheiros) left behind. Little endures of the dwellings, constructed in the open, made no doubt of nondurable material such as wood, branches, straw, and other segments of vegetation.

Mesolithic peoples who dwelt near the mouths of rivers or on the coast have left behind characteristic tools, for example, a kind of pick for prising shellfish from rocks and opening them and various microliths for use as harpoons, tridents and hooks. The large middens, or mounds of shells, fishbones and other debris accumulated over generations of inhabitants sometimes reached a height of five metres.

One of the most important Mesolithic sites is situated up the Tejo valley north of Lisboa about 80 kilometres where the shellmiddens of Muge were noted in 1863 and excavated intermittently from 1865 to 1892, from 1930 to 1937 and from 1951 to 1967. The graves there yielded numerous skeletons of men, women and children, and a definite funeral ritual—one of the most important finds for the period in the world. Most of the bodies were buried in the fetal position, covered in red ochre, and adorned with numerous shells around the neck or sometimes around the toes. Beside some graves, piles of unopened shells were placed, perhaps food for the journey to the land beyond.

One large midden, Cabeço da Arruda is 95 metres long, 40 metres wide and 5 metres deep and contained shellfish, bones of oxen, deer, sheep, horses, pigs and wild dogs, badgers and cats. Implements associated with the site were scrapers, microliths, and some bone tools. Of the five shellmidden sites here, only two still exist: Cabeço da Amoreira and Cabeço da Arruda. The overall chronological range for these sites is ca. 5400–3200 B.C.

Mesolithic cultures continued the traditions of the earlier Stone Age with some refinement in tools and perhaps more successive, or semi-permanent occupation of the same sites where conditions offered at least a seasonably favourable food supply. The Mesolithic period appears to have been prolonged in Central Portugal judging by the *concheiros* even after the appearance of Neolithic ceramics and the first megaliths of Reguengos de Monseraz. The overlap in dates between Late Mesolithic sites and those with early Neolithic pottery suggests a complex interaction of cultural behaviours that is not yet fully understood.

3. Neolithic Period

Neolithic or New Stone Age peoples (or at least their cultural characteristics) first appeared in Portugal in the south. They are mostly known from their cemeteries and style of pottery. Remains of Neolithic settlements, the first farmers and pottery producers, are not plentiful in the country nor is the process of Neolithicization (somewhat later here than along the Mediterranean) entirely understood. Neolithic communities, seem to have developed first along the Atlantic coasts, while in a second phase, their influence crept into the interior of the country. The process of change from Mesolithic food-gathering societies to Neolithic food-producing populations was a long and slow undertaking with many overlapping characteristics. The first signs such as polished stone and pottery seem to date back to the fifth millennium B.C. Animal domestication and the production of crops were delayed, appearing in the same region over the next two millennia. The earliest sites in the open air appear to be in the Algarve and Alentejo but burial sites in grottos of a comparable date are also found in Estremadura and further north around the mouth of the Mondego river. Neolithic pottery, animal bones and artifacts have been found at Olelas (Lisboa), Gruta da Furninha, Peniche (Leiria), Rio Maior (Santarém), Eira Pedrinha, Condeixa (Coimbra) and Lagos (Faro) among other places. So far only sparse remains have been found of these first agricultural communities along the Tejo river valley.

Typical of the first phase of the Neolithic is the cardial pottery or Impressed Ware, a type of ceramic introduced from the Mediterranean. Characteristic of the second phase is the lack of this type of ceramic and the use of other types of pottery as well as the construction of the first megalithic tombs.

Neolithic burials were generally in single cist-type graves or in caves until near the end of the period when the practice developed of placing the dead in communal ossuaries in a single chamber, either in a cave or an artificial megalithic structure such as a dolmen.

For further general reading pertaining to the Neolithic period see G. Barker, *Prehistoric Farming in Europe*. (Cambridge, 1985), J. Lewthwaite, The transition to Food Production: a Mediterranean perspective, in M. Zvelebil, ed., *Hunters in Transition*. (Cambridge, 1986), and A. Whittle, *Neolithic Europe: a survey* (Cambridge, 1985).

4. Megalithic Structures

Dolmens

Portugal abounds in megalithic necropoli in the form of dolmens, a type of collective tomb, often called in Portuguese, antas and sometimes orcas. The dolmens, along with other types of tombs, are associated with various artifacts of the Late Neolithic and Chalcolithic periods. The earliest seem to have been constructed about 4500 B.C.

Dolmens were used for the burial of the family or clan, sometimes over several generations. The most common type consists of a burial chamber constructed of large, flat upright stones and covered with a capstone forming the ceiling. Some have passages or entranceways made up of vertically placed slabs of stone and covered by other slabs forming a kind of tunnel into the burial chamber. The entire structure was covered over with earth forming a mound called, in Portugal, a mamoa. Dolmens with paintings or engravings on the stone occur but are more characteristic of the north of Portugal than the centre or south of the country.

Some investigators have suggested that the megalithic culture found in many parts of Europe stems from the western region of the Iberian peninsula, that is, Portugal, whence it was diffused eastward. Such views are based on the abundance of megaliths in the country and in many cases their great antiquity which seems to predate those existing elsewhere. This view is controversial, however, since some sites remain undated or questionable.

Several megalithic burial chambers near the Tejo valley and extending eastward toward Montemor-o-Novo seem to have been constructed by early pastoral-hunting peoples. Settlements in the area do not appear until about 2500 B.C. and it is thought that the megalithic tombs containing the bones of ancestors may have marked territorial boundaries of some early semi-nomadic clans.

Associated with the Upper Alentejo are over one thousand megalithic tombs which appear to have been in use at least until the middle of the third millennium B.C. In the area lying just north of Lisboa there are a number dating back to the fourth millennium B.C. which were employed as burial sites up to the close of the third millennium B.C. according to the artifacts associated with them. At the end of the fourth millennium B.C. the grave goods of the lower Tejo valley, the Lower Alentejo region, and the Algarve began to herald the Chalcolithic or Copper Age.

Seemingly two distinct cultural groups were among the early users of collective tombs in the area south of the Tejo. One was responsible for megalithic passage graves or dolmens and the other for round graves or tholos tombs. The megalithic tombs lie inland while the earliest of the tholoi are found along the coast.

Tholoi, Rock-cut tombs and cist graves

The early tholos type graves, beehive-shaped chambers built of stone and roofed by corbelling, were poor in metal artifacts but are found in close connection with copper ore deposits, and copper objects become plentiful in the later tombs of this cultural group. One such tomb may still be seen at Alcalar in the Algarve. The tholos tradition lasted for a considerable time in southern Portugal and western Andalucía and culminated in monuments such as the Cueva de Romeral near Antequera, Spain in the second millennium B.C.

The earliest of the southwestern tholos tombs seem to date back to a time not long after the middle of the fourth millennium B.C. In southern and central Portugal tholos tombs were still being built late in the third millennium B.C. and in the southern Alentejo the Anta dos Tassos (Ourique), with a dry-stone chamber and short passage, showed a radiocarbon date of ca. 1850 B.C.

Portuguese tholoi are mostly found in the Alentejo, the Algarve and the Lisboa peninsula. To the south of the Tejo twenty-six have been identified: twelve in the Algarve, ten in Baixo Alentejo and four in Alto Alentejo. Unfortunately, few have survived.

Rock-cut tombs or artificial grottos, dating from about 3000 to 2500 B.C., may be seen at various places in Estremadura such as Quinta do Anjo, Alapraia, Carenque (badly ruined), São Pedro do Estoril and near Torres Vedras (nearly destroyed). Cut from the rock, some of these monuments possessed a circular chamber rising to a vault or arched roof near the surface of the rock and are entered by a passageway or, more uniquely, by a circular manhole sealed by a stone slab which could be lifted to accommodate further burials. These original and specialized tombs form an interesting aspect of the late Neolithic and early Chalcolithic cultures in the Lisboa/Setúbal area. They appear to have been used by later peoples as well.

Cist graves are box-shaped burial structures made of stone slabs set on edge and placed below ground or on the surface, and covered over by a protective mound of earth. They appeared during Neolithic times and continued in use into the Bronze Age.

The Neolithic single burials south of the Tejo consisted of oblong or oval cists large enough to contain an extended corpse. They were built of small granite blocks laid upon the surface, roofed with corbelling and covered with circular mounds. The diffusion of the practice of communal burial seems to have provided the stimulus which caused these simple chambers to grow larger resulting in tholos type graves and dolmens. Once widespread, these vulnerable graves have suffered the ravages and destruction of agricultural implements and there are actually few now to see.

Menhirs

Menhirs are large, long and generally rounded stones embedded vertically in the ground. Various cultures at different times may have independently erected such stone structures. Many were phallic symbols of fecundity while others appear to have been of a commemorative nature indicating the existence of a nearby megalithic tomb or marking a boundary. The two purposes are not always distinguishable. Some had engravings. In Portugal they may be found throughout the country from the Algarve northward and, while difficult to date, appear to have been erected in the third millennium B.C. Some of the best preserved menhirs are to be found near Reguengos in the district of Évora.

Cromlechs

Cromlechs, stone circles in which the stones are often set on edge in the ground are common in the British Isles, but are also found in Portugal. For example, near Reguengos one surrounds a menhir and at another near Évora numerous large stones, not unlike scores of menhirs themselves, were implanted vertically in a clearing. These stone groupings appear sometimes to have been indicators of other nearby important monuments such as graves, or, at times they may have defined hallowed ground for religious or secular ceremonial practices.

5. Chalcolithic Period or Copper Age

While stonework continued the Neolithic traditions and a variety of amulets fashioned from stone included cylindrical stylized human figurines and model adzes, copper came to be employed for flat axes and daggers and a distinctive type of arrowhead with a near-circular blade and long tang. The settlements of these Copper Age peoples are illustrated by the site of Vila Nova de São Pedro (Santarém), where, upon the even earlier pre Copper Age settlement, fortifications were built, including an eight-metre-thick surrounding wall with semicircular bastions.

The distinctive types of concentric fortifications with bastions at Los Millares near Gádor in Almería, Spain, and Vila Nova de São Pedro have led some scholars to believe that early copper-using colonists responsible for these defenses came from the east sometime in the third millennium B.C. This position is now largely discredited.

Remains of Chalcolithic settlements may be seen at Zambujal near Torres Vedras, Vila Nova de São Pedro and Monte da Tumba near Torrão.

6. Bronze Age

This cultural period in Portugal seems to have begun about 1800 B.C. and by ca. 1000 B.C. the use of bronze was generalized throughout the country. Southern Portugal has always been rich in copper while the central and northern parts of the country contained substantial deposits of tin—the required element to make the alloy bronze. Bronze Age peoples were essentially pastoral, continuing the agricultural traditions of earlier times but they produced quantities of arms suggesting pastoral-warrior societies.

The Bronze Age is usually divided into phases of Initial (1800–1500 B.C.), Middle (1500–1200 B.C.) and Final 1200–700 B.C.) which naturally vary from region to region. South of the Tejo River the Early Bronze Age coincides with the gradual replacement of the old customs of communal burial among the indigenous megalith builders by one of single burial in cist graves.

Early phase

During the initial centuries of the Bronze Age, sites show burials in individual graves with arms, jewels and adornments in copper, gold and silver, and Bell Beaker pottery. Extensive necropoli consisting of cist graves were relatively frequent in the Algarve, Baixo Alentejo and the southern part of Alto Alentejo . Some have been found with skeletons (generally one to a grave but with exceptions) along with articles of bronze and clay pottery. The graves were rectangular, often made up of five stone slabs, one on each side, and a covering stone, but in the Algarve there were many exceptions. Measurements are roughly 0.90 metres to 1.50 metres length, 0.50 to 0.80 metres width, and 0.40 to 0.45 metres depth.

An important site is that of the cist graves of Ulmo (Santa Vitória, Beja) where a Bronze Age grave contained four skeletons, but here and at other such sites there is now little or nothing left to see. Another important site is the prehistoric monumental necropolis of Atalaia, situated next to Castro de Nossa Senhora da Cola, about eight kilometres from Aldeia dos Palheiros in the district of Ourique. As is often the case, the settlement to which the graves belonged has never been found.

Middle phase

The Middle Bronze period in Portugal has few defining characteristics that are not already present in the previous phase. However, the cemeteries do seem to indicate, at least in the south, the commencement of a new and more pronounced social order that would eventually be the basis of the complex societies of the Late Bronze period. During this time social structure evolved into more rigid or stratified forms as indicated by the grave goods. Also, during this period new settlements were developed on the coast without the benefit of natural defensive conditions, and where dependence on the sea for sustenance (fishing and shellfish collecting) appears to have become as important as agriculture.

Final phase

Further sophistication in metallurgy concerning production of arms and refinement of alloys and more intensive commercial interaction characterize the Final Bronze phase along with decorated grave stelae, for example, an engraved warrior holding a lance (ca. 900 B.C.), associated with a cist grave in the Algarve. These stones, often with swords, daggers and concentric circles embossed on them, seem to attest to a social hierarchy in which an upper or ruling class was more highly esteemed than the ordinary members of the society buried without such elaboration.

Some of the castros or hilltop villages of central and northern Portugal which were subsequently occupied by Iron Age peoples and later still by Romans seem to date back to the Final Bronze phase. The Castro da Senhora da Guia, Baiões, São Pedro do Sul, that seemingly ended violently around 700 B.C., appears to have been a Bronze Age settlement. Here were found bronze votive objects and smelting moulds. Similarly, in the Alentejo, walled settlements such as the Outeiro do Circo near Beringel (Beja) and Corõa do Frade near Nossa Senhora da Torega (Évora) attest to Bronze Age occupation.

The Bronze Age also seems to have been a period that ushered in much of the rupestrian decoration found in numerous places (many ancient sanctuaries) such as the engraved stone of Serrazes near São Pedro do Sul.

7. Pre-Roman Iron Age Peoples

During the first millennium before Christ, Indo-European peoples of presumably mostly Celtic stock, arrived on the Iberian peninsula from north of the Pyrenees. They occupied the sparsely populated central meseta while others pushed into the northwest and the Atlantic seaboard. Smaller numbers seem to have infiltrated the southwest where Bronze Age peoples, in contact with Phoenicians and Greeks, had already reached a relatively high level of civilization compared to their northern neighbours. The newcomers carried with them skills of iron-founding, animal herding, and practised cremation funeral rites.

Two phases of the Iron Age are usually distinguished in Europe: Phase I or Hallstatt period, named after the Austrian site, and Phase II or La Tène, the name of the type-site in Switzerland. The Hallstatt Celts appear to have occupied hilltop sites such as Briteiros in the sixth century B.C. and were at the zenith of their cultural development during the second phase in the fourth and third centuries B.C.

At Alcáçova de Santarém, along the Tejo valley, some remains of Iron Age occupation consisting of structures and silos were found dating back to the eighth century B.C. The site, much destroyed by subsequent Roman and Moslem habitation, also displays ceramic material similar to eastern Mediterranean cultures, probably relating to the first Phoenicians to arrive in the area.

Throughout Portugal the hilltop towns of the Celts, the citânias or castros as they are called, may number as many as five thousand, although relatively few are well-preserved. They are more numerous in the northern sections of the country. North of the Douro river over eight hundred have so far been accounted for. In the south where the Bronze Age lasted somewhat longer, Iron Age sites are less pronounced and Celtic influence less obvious.

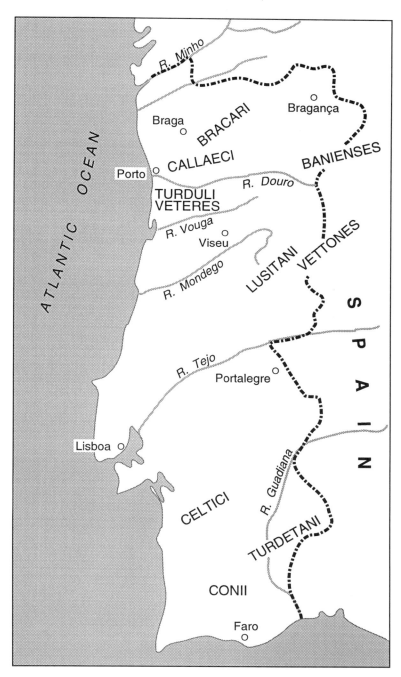

Map 3. Pre-Roman peoples of Portugal

11

Cultural and economic characteristics

The Iron Age Celtic peoples, the Lusitanians (a conglomerate of tribes), who gave their name to the region, seem to have occupied the area of the Serra da Estrêla in the district of Guarda where they lived, tending their flocks of sheep, in fortified castros encircling the tops of hills. These warrior-shepherds moved their flocks in winter to the more temperate lowlands and back into the highlands in spring and summer. They had few luxuries and led a more simple existence than many other peoples of ancient Portugal. According to artifacts found on location, they wove their own cloth on home-made looms. Diet consisted of meat from the flocks, fish, nuts, blackberries, milk and a variety of wheat grown locally and ground by hand-powered stone mills. They fermented their own type of beer. They made objects of bronze, iron and lead and sometimes silver and gold, and more rarely copper and tin, but not of a very high standard.

Several statues exist of Lusitanian warriors showing them dressed in short tunics wearing thick necklaces and bracelets and holding round shields. The ornaments were decorative as well as honorific and protective.

Some of the Celtic people of Portugal learned the Latin alphabet from the Romans and employed it to write their own language and, in some cases, documents were laboriously chiseled out of stone, a few of which are still extant and can be seen at Cabeço das Fráguas (Guarda) and Lamas de Moledo (Viseu). The decipherment of these inscriptions demonstrated the Indo-European character of the pre-Roman language of the castros and helped establish its relationship to other Celtic languages in Spain, Gaul and Britain. The stone of Lamas de Moledo appears to relate to the sacrifice of a bull, pig and sheep, invoking Celtic deities. The eastern neighbours of the Lusitanians were the Vettones, also of Celtic origin, who practised a cult involving the use of nearly life-size stone-sculptured animals in the shape of a boar or bull. This practice spread to some extent among the peoples of northern Portugal where such stone figures can still be seen in Murça (Vila Real), Bragança and Paredes de Beira (Viseu).

One of the survivors of a massacre of the Lusitanians by the Romans, Viriatus, rose as a popular resistance leader, gathered a force of shepherd-warriors and in 147 B.C. defeated a Roman army. Over the next several years he established control over a considerable area thwarting Rome's expansionist policy. His guerrilla tactics led to a series of Roman defeats and the twelve-year war was only brought to a close by his treacherous assassination.

Castros

Between the seventh century B.C. and the fourth or fifth centuries A.D. many places in the northern part of the country were occupied by Celtic villages or castros (from Latin *castrum* "a fortified camp or fort"). Hundreds of these sites, many in remote mountain areas and in various states of preservation, still exist today. For reasons of security the castros were built on defensible hilltops or high ridges usually above fertile valleys and near sources of metal, streams or rivers, and surrounded by one or more walls, oftentimes combined with moats. The circular stone houses (some were rectangular) with their conical straw roofs, were often constructed in clusters with a common patio and interior walls. With knowledge of iron metallurgy, agriculture, animal raising and fishing the population appears to have been self-sustaining. Some of the Celtic sites were inhabited by even earlier peoples, dating back to the Bronze Age or even Neolithic times, and after the Roman domination of the Iberian peninsula, many underwent Romanization as evidenced by the introduction of Roman inscriptions and coins and, in some cases, of Roman-style baths and aqueducts as, for example at Conimbriga. The exact nature of this cultural process of Romanization remains obscure but some castros were singled out by the Romans to serve as administrative centres in new organization of territory.

Distribution of pre-Roman peoples

Greek and Roman historiographers classified some of the tribes occupying ancient Lusitania and others are known from inscriptions. To the north of the Douro were the Callaeci, formed by two major groups: the Lucenses, mostly to the north of the Minho river and the Bracari to the south of it in the vicinity of Braga. To the east, where the river turns northeast along the Spanish border, dwelt the Banienses. The names of other tribes or clans are also known from regions north of Douro but in many cases that is all that is known.

South of the Douro and to the east in the Serra da Estrêla were the Lusitani whom the Romans came to know, perhaps better than they wished, along with their indomitable leader, Viriatus. Their eastern neighbours were the Vettones whose lands were primarily in present-day Spain. In the west, on the Atlantic coast on the south bank of the Douro in Beira Litoral, were the Turduli Veteres mentioned by Pliny and confirmed by two small plaques found at the Castro da Senhora Saúde (Vila Nova de Gaia), one of which is dated A.D. 7, the other A.D. 9. Still further south, the Celtici occupied the Alentejo and Guadiana basin. All of these tribes apparently were of Celtic origin.

Inscription from Southern Portugal

In the southernmost area the non-Celtic Conii or, as some Greek sources report, the Cynetes, had lived in the area probably since the Late Bronze Age. The name also seems to be recorded on tombstones from southern Portugal in an unknown language but employing a Graeco-Phoenician writing system dating from about the seventh to the fifth centuries B.C. (Some scholars prefer a later date.) The eighth and seventh century contacts with the Phoenicians mark the beginning of the Iron Age for the Conii as shown by their grave goods. While ancient authors place the Conii in the south, it is interesting to note that the city of Conimbriga, near Coimbra, contains the Celtic ending *-briga,* "oppidum or fortress," added to the name Conii suggesting "fortified city of the Conii."

Judging from ancient literary sources, the Celtici arrived in the Alentejo at the beginning of the fifth century B.C. and appear to have lived as neighbours to or among the Conii. There is some archaeological evidence (stamped pottery) for a second wave of Celts who arrived in the south in the third century B.C. Based on their names, the towns of Mirobriga, Lacobriga and Ebora must have been Celtic as well as Conistorgis (quoted in the classical sources but never found).

Besides the tribes or clans mentioned above whose names only tell part of the story, there were many others of perhaps lesser significance whose names appear on inscriptions from the Roman period or remain in the form of place names. Many smaller local tribes' names were sometimes recorded at specific places, such as a castro, but their larger affiliations are often not clear.

Religion

The inhabitants of pre-Roman Portugal worshipped many deities but unlike the Romans they did not generally erect temples and altars to them. They were venerated in rivers, woods, springs, craggy ravines or on the summits of mountains, places that are singularly unrevealing about the personality of the divinities. Only two constructed sanctuaries have been found to date: one at Mirobriga and another at Garvão. Recent excavations at Mirobriga, in the pre-Roman settlement area known as Castelo Velho which was an Iron Age oppidum, have unearthed a temple. Initially of the fourth century B.C., it was abandoned and re-used in the first and consisted of a small rectangular enclosure adjoining the outer rampart of the hill-fort. Literary sources refer to another at Cabo de São Vicente but no trace of it has been found. These sites in the south of the country were strongly influenced by Phoenician, Greek and Punic traders and colonists.

Rock shrines dating from Roman Imperial times are known at Panóias, Braga, Mogueira, Cabeço das Fráguas, Corgas Roçadas Lamas de Moledo, Sanfins, and Castro dos Três Rios among other places where votive inscriptions were carved in the living rock. Many refer to local divinities. Between the rivers Tejo and Douro about fifty such deities are known today, but only eight are known south of the Tejo in the Alentejo and none in the Algarve where foreign colonization was early and substantial. These sanctuaries owe their existence to Roman influence and the use of the Latin language or alphabet to inscribe the rock. The names of a few of the most widespread of these gods were Bandu and Cossu, seemingly male deities, Nabia, a goddess of valleys, hills, woods and flowing water, and Ataegina, a female, perhaps a goddess of the Celtic underworld. The ancient gods of Lusitania gradually disappeared with the introduction of Roman deities and the Imperial cult, with Christianity delivering the *coup de grâce*.

The vocabulary of inscriptional material and the remains of structures and artifacts suggest that, just prior to the arrival of the Romans, Celtic Lusitania was fairly uniform in language and culture.

For further reading concerning Paleolithic cultures down to the Iron Age see R.W. Chapman, *Emerging Complexity: The Later Prehistory of Southeast Spain, Iberia and the West Mediterranean.* (Cambridge, 1990), H. N. Savory, *Spain and Portugal: the Prehistory of the Iberian Peninsula* (London, 1968) and L.G. Straus, *Iberia Before the Iberians* (Albuquerque, 1992).

8. Phoenicians and Greeks

Phoenicians seeking tin and copper (in short supply in the east) as well as gold and silver, actively traded along the southern coasts of Portugal in the first half of the first millennium B.C., and established commercial centres. They competed for a time with Greek merchants who arrived in the sixth century B.C. When Phoenician power in the eastern Mediterranean slipped away, the mandate for exploitation in the western Mediterranean and beyond the Straits of Gibraltar passed to Carthage, a former colony of Phoenicia. By ca. 535, after the destruction of the Greek fleet at Alalia (Corsica), the Carthaginians remained in sole control of the area and its commercial enterprises in mining and fish curing.

North of the Portuguese Estremadura, Phoenician and Greek colonization made little impact and there is no evidence of settlements in this zone except some traces of Phoenician contact at the mouth of the Mondego river at Figueira da Foz. From the Tejo basin south, on the other hand, their influence is clear. Salacia, modern Alcácer do Sal, was a major centre of Phoenician and Greek activity, as recent archaeological finds illustrate, and the Algarve was decisively exploited. For example, Ossonoba, modern Faro, was probably of Phoenician origin. Much of the archaeological evidence comes from their industries and artifacts. In the north, about the same time, Celtic peoples were settling, building their hilltop villages or castros, and on occasion making incursions southward.

The southern portion of present-day Portugal, before the arrival of the Romans, was the most culturally advanced section of the country, probably due to Tartessian influence as well as to that of Phoenicians, Greeks and Carthaginians. Just before the middle of the first millennium B.C., the Tartessians (also known as the Turdetani), whose cities and towns have not been found but whose presence is known from classical written sources and artifacts such as treasure hoards, ornaments and weapons, appear to have had significant influence in the southwest of the peninsula. They seem to have been an important trading block but their civilization, probably centred in western Andalucía in the vicinity of Huelva or along the Guadalquivir river near Cádiz, vanished after the sixth century B.C. with the surge of Punic power in the area. That they may have established themselves in southern Portugal at some uncertain date is suggested by the terminations *-oba* and *-ip(p)o* as in Ossonoba, Olisipo and Collipo—forms that are also found on coins in southwest Spain as *-uba,* compare with Corduba (modern Córdoba) and Onuba (modern Huelva).

The archaeological record shows a profound transformation in the fifth and fourth centuries B.C. in the Algarve and Lower Alentejo occasioned, it would seem, by the decline of Tartessian power and the arrival of Celtic tribes who began to fill the vacuum. Incineration of the dead became the practice and writing disappeared. Hellenistic and other eastern Mediterranean contacts faded away as the Carthaginians, now in the ascendancy, closed the Straits of Gibraltar to foreign commerce.

Carthaginian activity and occupation in the southern part of Portugal before the arrival of the Romans is not well-documented. It is clear, however, that in 210 B.C. a Carthaginian army, commanded by Mago, was in the Algarve and another, commanded by Hasdrubal, was stationed at the mouth of the river Tejo. The earliest coins found in the area of the Tejo river are not Roman but Hispano-Carthaginian, minted in the third century B.C. These finds, coupled with contemporary written documentation, demonstrate the presence of Carthaginian troops in the area at the time of the Second Punic War (218–202 B.C.).

9. Roman Lusitania

The Iberian peninsula as a whole passed to Roman hands as a result of the Second Punic War between Rome and Carthage. Roman occupation of the Alentejo and the Algarve took place sometime between 202 B.C. (the end of the Second Punic War) and 139 B.C., when Quintus Servilius Caepio established a camp in the lands of the Celtici. The details of this early conquest are sparse compared to the accounts relating to the Lusitanian wars fought in the north.

With the capitulation of Cádiz, a Carthaginian town and headquarters, it is probable that southern Portugal was given up without a fight. The southern peoples, more refined and less bellicose than their northern neighbours, were easily subdued by the legions. At least there is no account of fierce opposition. The north was a different matter where Celtic resistance to Roman hegemony was fierce and prolonged and where a general uprising in the Serra da Estrêla under Viriatus gathered strength throughout much of the peninsula (see also Pre-Roman Iron Age Peoples).

The Romans wasted little time conquering the plain of the Ribatejo and the coastal lowlands north of the river Mondego but the interior of the country, girdled by windswept mountain ranges, was the main theatre of war between the legions and the Lusitanians.

Military campaigns

The conquest of central Portugal began in 138 B.C. when the Consul Decimus Iunius Brutus established a camp at Lisboa (Olisipo) and embarked on a campaign to pacify the northwest of the peninsula. As he moved northward, the Lusitanian strongholds were destroyed in and around the Serra da Estrêla, and a fortified camp was established on the plateau at Viseu. This camp, the so-called Cava de Viriato, the largest yet known in Portugal and unlike any other, afforded the Romans easy access to the coast along the valleys of the Mondego and Vouga rivers. Crossing the Douro, the Consul then marched to the Lima, proceeded to the Minho and into present-day Galicia. (The route and the date of the camp are, however, controversial.) A Roman stronghold was also established at Santarém. The construction of Roman roads, bridges and rustic villas soon followed.

When serious social upheavals transpired in Rome, Quintus Sertorius, attempted to restore the fortunes of the Marian party (a Roman political party led by Marius) in Spain (80 B.C.). He achieved personal leadership of the rebellious Lusitanians but, like Viriatus, the Roman general was eliminated through assassination.

In 61 B.C. Lisboa became the headquarters of Julius Caesar. Colonists were settled at Santarém (Scallabis), Braga (Bracara Augusta), and the town of Beja (Pax Iulia) was founded.

In 27 B.C., Hispania Ulterior was divided by Augustus into Baetica, now Andalucía, and Lusitania which corresponded to modern Portugal south of the Douro river and Spanish Extremadura. The capital was Augusta Emerita (Mérida) on the Guadiana River.

Between the Douro and the Minho rivers the north became the administrative unit (*conventus bracarum*) of the province of Tarraconensis which was created in 2 B.C. and which in the third century was combined with the northwest corner of the peninsula to form the province of Gallaecia.

The long, drawn-out conquest of Portugal was finally terminated during the reign of Augustus, nearly two hundred years after the Romans had first landed on the Iberian peninsula.

Roman towns

The Romans moved into and took over many pre-existing towns, especially in the Algarve and along the Atlantic seaboard, and in other places they started from scratch and laid out the town to their own specifications. The archaeological record is not always clear which was the case, especially in built-up areas where extensive excavation is not feasible. Braga shows no indication of a previous Iron Age settlement while Lisboa was clearly built around a pre-Roman oppidum on the hill of Castelo de São Jorge as archaeological finds and the ancient name, Olisipo, indicate.

The choices of location of Roman settlements were often based on practical and economic considerations. For example, Alcácer do Sal (ancient Salacia) became important for the production of salt and Aljustrel, ancient Vipasca, for copper ore and silver. Further inland, Évora and Beja developed into important centres of an extensive agricultural belt. The southern coastal cities of Faro and Tavira (ancient Balsa) were significant ports and centres of the fishing industry. The geographical location of Viseu, crisscrossed by several ancient roads, gave it a special importance while other sites, such as the somewhat isolated Romanized Iron Age hilltop settlements of Briteiros and Sanfins, did not persist and develop as towns or cities. They were abandoned in the third or early fourth centuries of the Christian era when the inhabitants of these fortified settlements no longer felt compelled to seek protection in mountain strongholds since more prosperous advantages could be obtained under the Roman peace in the cities.

Economic factors

The Romans quickly took charge of the economy of ancient Lusitania which was based primarily on agricultural pursuits along with other important industries such as mining and fish products.

Along the coasts, especially in the Sado and Tejo estuaries, and in the south, the production of the fish sauce, garum, along with other kinds of marine products and preserves such as salted fish, were some of the most important industries of the entire country. These products were exported to all parts of the Empire.

The Romans and the local inhabitants also engaged in many other economic activities including the manufacture of building materials such as terracotta roofing tiles, dressed stone, and plaster. Pottery-making was carried out at Braga and elsewhere. Other activities included the production of oil lamps and amphoras. Wool garments and linens were made, often home-spun, a fact which is demonstrated by the loom weights and spindle whorls found in many excavations.

In at least one place, the Aljustral mining area, the employment of trades was exercised as a monopolistic enterprise during the reign of Trajan or Hadrian and the concessionary paid a fee to the state for the privilege. For example, a man might have one or several shops for producing, dyeing or washing cloth in which he employed slaves or salaried freedmen, and he might even sublet. Unless prices were already set by a state official he could control the costs of goods and services. For this, the state exacted a fee. Similarly, only a shoe-maker under license could make or repair shoes (unless they were homemade) and anyone caught producing illegal footwear for sale was fined double the amount of the sale which was then given to the shoe concessionary.

Mining

Portugal was an important mining centre in Roman times and even earlier for gold, copper, lead, tin and iron. The mines at Aljustrel, for example, were worked as far back as the Chalcolithic and Bronze Age, according to artifacts discovered at the site. Mining was intensive from the Augustan age to the third century A.D. and continued through the fourth and fifth centuries.

Two bronze tablets recovered from the Roman mine at Aljustrel record some of the legislation pertaining to the operation of the mine. The right to mine was obtained by paying a tax which granted permission to open a new shaft within twenty-five days of signing the contract. The concession was lost if the time elapsed. The concessionary had to pay the state one half of the ore extracted from the mine. Transportation of the ore at night from the mine to the foundries was forbidden, and severe penalties were meted out to those caught stealing or moving goods clandestinely. There were regulations that covered technical aspects of shoring up the shafts and galleries, their maintenance, minimum distance between shafts and the use of drainage channels.

During Roman times the most important mines were Aljustrel (mainly for copper and some silver), Três Minas (for gold) and São Domingos (for copper). While many mining sites are in evidence in Portugal there is precious little left for the general visitor to appreciate. There is a small, but interesting, mining museum at Aljustrel.

Roman villas and mosaics

The backbone of agriculture in ancient Lusitania were the estates or country villas which were often farms producing cereals, olive oil, wine and livestock. The rolling hills and plains of the Alentejo, as one might expect, contained many such farms. The villas are also the best places to see mosaics as many had proprietors rich enough to afford the artists and craftsmen to make them. Mosaics may be in black and white with geometric designs or, as in the more affluent villas, polychrome motifs of famous classical scenes.

The eastern part of the Alentejo, especially around Beja, is rich in mosaics, as is the Algarve, while there are fewer such works of art in the land to the north of the Mondego or the inland region between the Tejo and the Douro. The paucity of mosaics in the north of the country appears due to the dearth of wealthy Roman country houses.

The many villas that once existed in the vicinity of Lisboa have mostly disappeared under the expansion of urban sprawl, and many other Roman sites in the Tejo valley have been obliterated by agriculture and the meanderings of the river.

Most villas were devoted to agricultural interests and may display storage silos, outbuildings and earthen dams but others, especially those near the sea, sometimes specialized in marine products and the vats for fish curing and production of garum are often still in evidence. The remains of baths and requisite water and heating systems in villas are frequently evident such as those at Torre de Palma (where two baths are known), Pisões, Milreu, São Cucufate and Cerro da Vila.

Public baths

Public baths were popular institutions throughout the Roman Empire and were enjoyed by every level of society. They were places for social interaction and business activity as well as for hygienic practices and were constructed around natural hot springs or else had water piped to them that was heated by furnaces. Most had the advantage of cold (frigidarium), tepid (tepidarium) and hot (caldarium) water pools along with changing rooms.

They are known at numerous places in Portugal such as Braga, Freixo (Marco de Canaveses), São Vicente do Pinheiro and São Pedro do Sul. Excavations at Conimbriga have revealed four public baths and one associated with a private house while others are found at Mirobriga and Tróia.

With the decline of the Empire and the influx of barbarian tribes, the baths fell into disuse and decay. Some were even destroyed. Bathing was considered too effete for the warrior and the practice of enjoying the benefits of the bath was only revived under Moslem rule.

Roman roads, bridges and dams

Ancient roads and bridges are not always possible to identify as Roman and may in some cases be Medieval constructions built in the Roman style. The roads presented here give the main towns and cities with their modern names and omit the numerous connecting roads and bridges many of which have disappeared or are uncertain.

A major road from Lisboa went north to Santarém and on to Tomar, Conimbriga, Coimbra, Cabeço do Vouga, Monte de Santa Maria and to Braga and eventually to the Portela do Homem and Astorga in Spain. From Braga another road went east to Chaves continuing to Castro de Avelãs. From Cabeço do Vouga a major road headed eastward to Viseu and then southeast to Idanha-

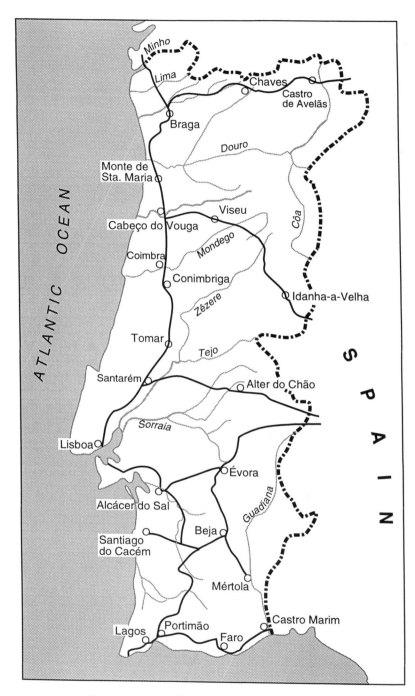

Map 4. Some of the Roman roads of Lusitania

a-Velha and into Spain. Another headed east from Santarém to Alter do Chão then to Augusta Emerita in Spain. An important road connected Mértola with Beja and Évora to the north. From the Roman capital at Mérida it was possible to reach Lisboa via the road to Évora then to Alcácer do Sal and on to Lisboa. Along the southern coast there was a road from Castro Marim to Faro and Portimão and on to Lagos and beyond. From the vicinity of Portimão a road went north, branching right toward Beja and left to Santiago do Cacém or continued northward to Alcácer do Sal. There were hundreds of connecting roads and branch roads to more remote locations such as mining towns.

Some of the better places to view, and perhaps to walk along a Roman road are at Almargem (Viseu), Galhardos (Guarda) and Portela do Homem (Braga).

Roman bridges and milestones are good indicators of where Roman roads once were even if they no longer exist. While there were many milestones in the country a fair number of them have been moved to museums. The best places to see them today in their original locations are at the Portela do Homem or along the Roman road in the Gerês Park. Bridges, on the other hand, tend to remain in situ. Of the numerous Roman bridges in the country the most outstanding is that at Vila Formosa, a long, heavy-duty structure having many large arches with smaller arches between them. Other good examples of Roman engineering are the bridge at Ponte de Pedra (reconstructed) and the one at Chaves. The latter, on the road that linked Braga and Astorga, contains inscriptional pillars.

Where it was necessary to preserve water, especially in regions of low rainfall and sometime streams such as in the Alentejo, the Romans built dams, and some of these still exist. Particularly frequent south of the river Tejo where some twenty are known, three dams are in the vicinity of Beja and another half-dozen or so southeast of Portalegre, but they were constructed in all sections of the country. Generally made of dirt, stones or bricks, they were often associated with villas where a controlled system of water was needed for the baths as well as for agricultural use. Many of these dams are still little explored and unexcavated.

Amphitheatres, theatres, circuses and temples

Amphitheatres are rare in Portugal. There are two in the process of excavation: one at Conimbriga and another at Bobadela. Another, at Braga, was still visible in the eighteenth century but has since disappeared.

Theatres and circuses are equally few and far between. Only two theatres are known so far and one of those, at Évora, is not definite. The other is in Lisboa. At Mirobriga the remains of a circus measuring 360 by 76 metres are still visible, and another at Tavira is only known from inscriptions.

Of the many Luso-Roman temples that must have once existed in Portugal, only that of Évora preserves part of the colonnades. The frieze and mosaic floor have disappeared completely. In the Praça da República in Beja there once existed the remains of a temple partially excavated in 1939 but nothing is left in situ. There was another in Faro that has also disappeared.

In the acropolis of Mirobriga near Santiago do Cacém some remnants of a temple are preserved, with four columns of the façade and the platform. Another apsidal structure nearby was apparently a temple dedicated to Venus. At Santana do Campo, Arraiolos, there are some partially preserved walls of a temple incorporated into the eighteenth century church and above the town of Orjais, Castelo Branco, are the remains of a temple with only the podium still in evidence. Near Figueira de Castelo Rodrigo are the foundations of Casarão da Torre, somewhat rebuilt in later centuries.

Funeral practices

Incineration was the normal funeral rite employed by the pre-Roman Celtic cultures of ancient Portugal. For those in high position it could be an elaborate affair such as the inurnment of Viriatus who, according to a Roman account, was dressed in magnificent robes and cremated on a lofty pyre. Warriors danced around the flames reciting eulogies and sacrificing animals after which they held mock battles over the ashes. The urns containing the ashes of the dead were sometimes placed in houses or sometimes outside by the town walls. They were sometimes put in small pits surrounded by stones which may have served for more than one burial.

In Roman times incineration continued to be the general practice at least up until the middle of the third century A.D. The ashes were either thrown to the wind or deposited in glass, clay or marble urns. Sometimes a coin was interred with the ashes to pay the passage to the other world, but this was not common in Lusitania. The urn and funerary objects were placed in holes which may or may not have been covered over with a stone. Sometimes the ashes were put in a stone or lead box. From the second century A.D. onwards, epitaphs usually began with the formula *d.m.s.* for *diis manibus sacrum*, that is, consecrated "to the sacred Gods of Manes" and followed by the name, affiliations and age of the deceased. Often the names were also given of the relatives who ordered the stone incised with the epitaph. The inscription would then terminate with the abbreviations *h.s.e. hic situs est*, or *s.t.t.l. sit tibi terra levis* "May the earth rest lightly on you." The practice of inhumation appears to have become generalized in the fourth century A.D. in the wake of expanding Christian beliefs.

Decline and legacy of Roman Lusitania

In the middle of the second century A.D. the southern part of the Iberian peninsula suffered attacks by Moors from Mauritania. Although Lusitania was not greatly affected by these incursions from across the Straits of Gibraltar there is some inscriptional evidence that there was concern about the security of the mines at Aljustrel. Similarly, during the barbarian incursions of Franks and Alans southward in the years between ca. A.D. 260–280, Lusitania appears to have escaped a direct attack but coin hoards buried during these twenty years suggest a period of great insecurity. The Suevi, Alans and Vandals invaded the peninsula in earnest in A.D. 409 taking advantage of the conflict and civil war between the Roman Emperor of the west, Honorius, and Constans. The ensuing period was one of breakdown of authority, turmoil and devastation.

After over four centuries of rule, the Roman legacy in the form of in situ physical remains can be well appreciated at the towns of Conimbriga, Évora,

Mirobriga, Idanha-a-Velha, Bobadela, Freixo and Tróia, at numerous villas such as Torre de Palma, Milreu, São Cucufate, Cerro da Vila and from the network of roads, milestones and bridges. The museums contain Roman statues, tombstones, inscriptions and artifacts. On a less tangible note, their greatest legacy was the Latin language and culture which shaped the foundations of the modern country in spite of centuries of Moslem rule. The Portuguese language is a continuation of the Latin brought to Lusitania by the soldiers, merchants and farmers who settled there and whose descendants have called it home.

The social, economic and political cohesion of the Roman empire served as the vehicle for the rapid spread of Christianity throughout Europe. During the fourth century the Roman emperors repressed Christianity, then tolerated it, and finally embraced it. In the last century of Roman rule, bishoprics were established at Braga, Évora, Faro and Lisboa. Christian doctrines were already clearly established in parts of present-day Portugal before the Council of Elvira in Spain at the end of the third or beginning of the fourth century since it was attended by, among others, the bishops of Évora and Ossonoba (or Faro). The first known bishop of Olisipo, that is, Lisboa, held office as early as A.D. 357 and that of Braga in A.D. 400. When the security of the Roman world collapsed and the Germanic Suevi ruled in Lusitania, they came as pagans but in time converted to the faith of the inhabitants.

For a comprehensive account of Roman Portugal and a succinct treatment of pre-Roman Lusitanian tribes see Jorge de Alarcão, *Portugal Romano*, 4th rev. ed. Historia Mundi, Vol. 33 (Lisbon, 1987), and *Roman Portugal, Vols. 1 and 2,* (Warminster, 1988). For a treatment of prehistory down through Roman times see Vítor de Oliveira, Jorge et al., *Nova História de Portugal, Vol. I, Portugal—Das Origens A Romanização* (Lisboa, 1990).

10. Barbarian Tribes

With the invasion from beyond the Pyrenees in A.D. 409 by major groups of barbarian tribes (Vandals, Suevi and Alans), the Asding Vandals and Suevi settled in the northwest and the Siling Vandals in the south, today Andalucía. The Suevi, sometimes called Swabians, occupied the regions of Galicia and the land between the Minho and Douro rivers, while the Alans took up residence in the Roman province of Lusitania to the south. Entering the peninsula on behalf of Rome, the Visigoths defeated the Alans and the Siling Vandals scattering the former and annihilating the latter before returning to Gaul.

War broke out in the northwest between the Suevi and the Asding Vandals and with the help of a Roman army, the Vandals were defeated but allowed to settle in Baetica taking the place of their cousins who had been effaced from history two years earlier. In A.D. 429 they crossed the Straits to North Africa and eventually established their short-lived kingdom in the former territory of ancient Carthage. They were vanquished by a Byzantine army which also restored Imperial rule along the southern coasts of the Iberian peninsula, including the Algarve, in A.D. 554.

The Suevi had reached the northwest of the peninsula as early as A.D. 411 and had developed a substantial kingdom. Although apparently few in numbers, by the middle of the fifth century (the peak of their Hispanic empire) they controlled Galicia and Lusitania along with, for a time, some eastern sections of Baetica. The demise of the Suevi was nearly as rapid as their growth. Internal dissension and prolonged warfare deprived them of strength and they were eventually subdued by the Visigoths and disappeared from the historical record near the end of the sixth century A.D. Their history is obscure with little documentary evidence. A chronicle written by the bishop of Chaves, Hydatius, is the only contemporary account of the Suevi.

The Visigoths re-entered the Iberian peninsula after having been defeated in Gaul by the Franks in A.D. 507 and they eventually established their capital at Toledo. The most southerly of the Portuguese provinces, the Byzantine territory of the Algarve, fell to the Visigoths in A.D. 629.

The northwestern kingdom of the Suevi seems to have been incorporated by the Visigothic monarchy with the subsequent fusion of their respective aristocracies. Although not strong in the western and northwestern parts of the peninsula, Visigothic influence nevertheless went unchallenged until the Moslem invasions from North Africa.

11. Early Christian and Visigothic Art and Architecture

In the last years of the fourth century Lusitania, along with other regions of the peninsula, was embroiled in the turmoil surrounding the popular heretical doctrine of Priscillianism, a cult that may have had its roots in Galicia. The heresy was antitrinity, denied the resurrection of the body, and sought equality of women in the church. Its leader, Priscillian, suffered a martyr's fate and the sect faded away after denunciation at the Council of Braga around the year 563. It left no lasting memorials.

Some monuments of Visigothic origin are preserved in Portugal but apparently there was a period of transition during the development of late Roman and Visigothic times in which Paleo-Christian themes appeared, for example on a unique sarcophagus discovered in the cathedral at Braga which seems to date back to the fifth century A.D. On the frontal side of the sarcophagus is a krater or vase out of which arise stems or branches and beside which birds are depicted pecking at grapes. On each end is a monogram with the letters alpha and omega within a crown of laurel. A second krater and roses are found on the other side of the sarcophagus.

In the sixth century, artistic sentiments were expressed in architectural decorations and small pieces of art but in the next century there was a change in these endeavours manifested in new forms of Visigothic architecture such as the horseshoe arch and decorated pilasters and capitals that have a special and unique place in European art. Early Christian and Visigothic monuments and ornamentation in situ may be seen at Conimbriga, Idanha-a-Velha, Marmelar, Mértola, Milreu, Montinho das Laranjeiras, Odrinhas, Pisões, São Frutuoso de Montélios, São Gião de Nazaré, São Pedro de Balsemão, Sines, Torre de Palma, and Tróia.

12. Moslem Conquest and Christian Reconquest

With the Moslem assault from North Africa in the year 711, the invaders fanned out over the peninsula and by 713 had incorporated the old Roman province of Lusitania into their domain. There seems to have been little concerted effort to establish Moslem society in the northwest of the peninsula and only a few garrisons were situated north of the Mondego river valley.

In the initial phases of the reconquest during the decade of the 740's, Christian forces secured Galicia and then drove south occupying at least temporarily the Minho region and beyond to the lower Douro. However, the Christian communities of the northwest lacked the resources at the time to control effectively the lands south of the Minho.

The Moslems struck back in a number of bloody campaigns in the latter half of the eighth century and for some time, much of northern Portugal remained a ravaged land of burnt-out towns and half-deserted countryside, an impoverished frontier area.

Mozarabs

The situation changed in the ninth century with the influx of Mozarabs, Christians living under Arab domination, from the south, and resettlement under Christian jurisdiction, arranged by counts appointed by the king Alfonso I of Asturias-León. Late in the ninth century the territory south of the Lima river and north of the Douro was detached from Galicia—an area sufficiently pacified—and entrusted to a governor. Its seat was the town of Portucale, near the mouth of the Douro river, which later would lend its name to the entire country, becoming an important centre of administration. By the end of the century the region was no longer considered a frontier area. As the Christians moved southward, one town after another fell into their hands such as Coimbra in 878, then Viseu and Lamego.

Again the Moslems rebounded, however, and destruction and devastation reappeared as battle lines seesawed back and forth. The King of León, Ordoño III, raided Lisboa in 955 and further systematic campaigns followed in the late tenth century. The powerful Moslem chief, al-Mansur, struck as far north as Galicia in vicious attacks and re-established the frontier along the banks of the Douro. Only about seventy years later were the battle-hardened Christians able to reach Coimbra again and hold the line along the Mondego river. Lamego was definitively reconquered in 1057, Viseu in 1058 and Coimbra in 1063.

The Moslems called the flourishing regions west and northwest of the Guadiana river al-Gharb al-Andalus "the west of Andalus." As their territory contracted under pressure from Christian armies, al-Gharb shrank to the strip of land now called the Algarve. When in the eleventh century the central Moslem authority in Córdoba collapsed, there appeared all over the Moslem south petty kingdoms known as Taifas (from Arabic *tawa'if* "party" or "banner"). Six of these rose and fell in al-Gharb al-Andalus between 1012 and 1094.

Almoravides and Almohades

Threatened by Christian advances, some of the Taifas of the southern Iberian peninsula called on the Almoravides of North Africa for assistance. The whole of al-Gharb fell into their hands and the Moslem frontier was pushed north again to the Mondego basin. The Almoravide victory over the Christian forces in 1092–1094 brought about unification of the south once more. But as unity broke down, the Taifas reappeared and the North African Almohades were again called in to protect the Moslem south. Like the Almoravides, they came from Morocco and were religious fanatics who found the Almoravides debauched and heretical, although they, too, had begun as reforming zealots. Islamic internal dissension continued and Christian forces made new inroads into the south.

For a broad study of Moslem Portugal see Jan Read, *The Moors in Spain and Portugal* (London, 1974).

13. Birth of the Nation

Alfonso I of Castile, a warrior king, captured Toledo from the Moslems in 1085. His younger daughter, Teresa, was married in 1095 to count Henry of Burgundy, one of a number of French knights who had won the king's gratitude for assistance in the subjection of the city. As dowry Teresa received the lands south of the river Minho, the acknowledged frontier of Galicia. The new county was to be under the strict suzerainty of Castile.

Henry of Burgundy became Count of Portucale, but after his death, his widow Teresa acted as regent during the minority of her son, Afonso Henriques. The son of Teresa and Henry of Burgundy had his own plans for the county of Portucale. Wresting power from his mother and profiting from turbulence in Castile, he waged his own conquest southward against the Moslems. In 1139 Afonso Henriques won a victory over the Moslems near Santarém, secured northern Portugal, and proclaimed himself king of an independent country.

After a number of trials and tribulations, he eventually achieved the sought-after recognition of the kingdom from his cousin Alfonso VII in 1143, and later from the Pope. Portugal had become a nation. As Afonso I, the Conqueror, King of Portugal, and to the Moslems Ibn-Arrik, the Cursed of Allah, he took possession of Santarém in 1147 and after a seventeen-week siege, Lisboa was captured with the help of English, German and Flemish crusaders originally bound for the Holy Land.

By the end of the reign of Afonso I, Évora had fallen into Christian hands and further sweeping advances were made southward into Moslem territory. Afonso I's successors were burdened with the tasks of defending their territory, capturing the Alentejo and the Algarve from the Almohades, rebuilding the war-devastated regions of the country, fending off the ambitions of the nobility and claimants to the throne, and disputing with the church for land, money (taxes) and power.

It was left to Afonso III, who reigned 1248–1279, to conquer the province of al-Gharb in 1249 with a joint Portuguese-Castilian army. The Portuguese reconquest was complete. A frontier with Castile was then established along the Guadiana river and the current borders of Portugal, except for some minor details, were established. Today, the great Arabic castles at Sintra and Silves are poignant reminders of Moslem domination of bygone centuries.

For further reading see R. Collins, *Early Medieval Spain, Unity in Diversity 400–1000* (London, 1983), H.V. Livermore, *A New History of Portugal* (Cambridge, 1967), Damião Peres *Como nasceu Portugal* (Porto, 1967) and A. H. de Oliveira Marques, *History of Portugal, Vol. I, From Lusitania to Empire* (New York and London, 1972).

14. Luso-Jewish Communities

It is far from clear when the first Jews arrived in Portugal or indeed in the Iberian peninsula. That they may have come as merchants in the time of Solomon or as fugitives from the reign of Nebuchadnezzar must remain in the realm of speculation. Not until the third century A.D. is there written documentation indicating their presence in Portugal and not until the fourth century do we have the oldest vestige, in the form of a funerary stone from Espiche, near Lagos.

During the hegemony of the Visigoths, the Jews became more prominent, sometimes protected by the kings who coveted their wealth and sometimes persecuted in times of Christian fanaticism. During the centuries of Christian reconquest of the land from the Moslems, the Jews fought sometimes for one side, sometimes for the other, but all the while forming communities in various parts of the country such as at Lisboa and Santarém. Under Christian domination their lives vis-à-vis their pious neighbours were regulated by royal edicts. For example, they were prohibited to have a Christian servant under penalty of losing all their possessions, or to occupy important official posts. Once having converted to the Christian faith, a return to Judaism assured the death penalty.

In effect they became the property of the king's will, referred to in royal parlance as "My Jews," and were subject to his benevolence or animosity. There was little fear of rebellion if the king chose to make their lives miserable since their numbers were relatively small among the total population and the people in general, along with the church, supported persecution of non-Christian minorities. In spite of much adversity, Jewish communities, or Judiarias, developed in many cities and towns where they lived in their own quarters around their synagogues.

Alfamas

By the time Dom Denis (reigned 1279–1325) was on the throne of Portugal, Jewish communities were widespread throughout the country although, in many cases, they consisted of only a few families. The alfamas or Jewish quarters recorded in the documents of his reign were at Lisboa, Santarém, Bragança, Évora, Viseu, Coimbra, Mogadouro, Monforte, Rio Livre, Castelo Rodrigo, Chaves, Olivença, Guarda, and Faro. Others existed or were soon to come into being at Porto, Setúbal, Guimarães, Belmonte, Leiria, Beja, Silves and Loulé.

According to the available records from the thirteenth and fourteenth centuries on, individual Jews (with their biblical names such as Moisés, Isaac, Abraão, Judas, Jacob, Simão, David, Salomão, and José) practised a variety of professions or occupations. Some of the more common were physician, attorney, miller, weaver, tailor, dyer, baker, smithy, merchant, butcher, grocer, notary, buttonmaker, shoemaker, lacemaker, and goldsmith. There are only rare examples of Jewish farmers.

The expulsion of the Jews from Spain in 1492 increased the Luso-Hebreo population but for many their sojourn in Portugal was short-lived and they were again ordered, during the reign of Dom Manuel II (1495–1521), to convert to Christianity or leave the kingdom. In 1496, in order to marry Isabel, eldest daughter of Fernando and Isabella of Spain, Manuel accepted the Spanish condition that he expel the Jews and Moslems from Portugal. He first tried a policy of forcible conversion of the Jews to Christianity but many left for distant lands such as Holland, England and Germany. Under the circumstances, synagogues were demolished or transformed into churches, Jewish property was confiscated and their cemeteries were destroyed and used for pasture land, or built over.

Another heavy blow fell on the Jews remaining in the country in 1506 when public intolerance reached a peak and in spite of having become new Christians, they were massacred in the streets and in their homes in Lisboa. The plague, infesting the city at the time, was equated with the activities of heretics and the Dominican monks, clamouring for retribution, fired the mobs with hate. Living and dead alike were burned in improvised conflagrations in the streets. But, in spite of everything, some Jews continued to practise their rites in secret.

The Inquisition

The writing was on the wall for the converted Jews with the implacable animosity of Dom João III (reigned 1521–1557), and his anti-Semitic parliament. The Inquisition was established in Portugal to prosecute those caught keeping the faith of their ancestors, and secret societies created to hunt down those who relapsed.

Into the eighteenth century converted Jews still suffered the penalty of death by burning, the last victim being sentenced in 1739. The Inquisition lost much of its power after this as the government prohibited these extreme acts of punishment. The building belonging to the Inquisition disappeared in the earthquake of 1755 and by the end of the century the Holy Office of the Inquisition had itself disappeared under a series of government edicts banning its functions. By the nineteenth century Jews, both the survivors and new immigrants, were free to practise their religion, build synagogues and bury their dead in Jewish cemeteries. Besides a physical presence left behind by the Jews in the form of their homes and temples, they also left some interesting characteristics in the Portuguese vocabulary.

In its struggle to eradicate pagan influence from society and the language, Christianity had a triumph with Sunday as Dies Dominica which became *domingo* (the day of the Lord). Not so successful with Saturday, they accepted Hebrew sabbath as *sábado*, probably from the variant sabbatum. However, the Latin Dies Saturni (the day of Saturn), was still found on tombstones in the fifth century A.D. They were not able to supplant the other days of the week with Christian forms but again borrowed from the Jews by calling each day of the week a *feria* and giving it a number. For example, about A.D. 400, Saint Augustine wrote *quarta feria* for Wednesday. This system of the days of the week has persisted only in Portuguese among the Romance languages.

The places where something tangible may still be seen of the Medieval Jewish quarters in Portugal are Castelo de Vide and Tomar (the best sites), and Belmonte and Guarda.

For a thorough study of the Jews in Portugal see Maria José Pimenta Ferro, *Os Judeus em Portugal no Século XIV* (Lisbon, 1979) and, by the same author, *Os Judeus em Portugal no Século XV*, Vol. 1 (Lisbon, 1982).

15. Ceramic Material

Of the various types of ceramic material or pottery found in ancient Portugal which help date sites, three stand out for their affiliations with cultural epochs and their universally known characteristics:

Cardial or Impressed Ware

A simple type of decorated pottery produced by impressing a design into the clay when still soft, it is associated with the first Neolithic farmers who often decorated their pottery with the serrated edge of the cardium or cockleshell. It spread around the central and western Mediterranean between ca. 5000–3500 B.C. but its origins have proven elusive with no obvious eastern source.

Bell Beaker

Shaped like an inverted bell, this type of pottery is a drinking vessel associated primarily with Copper and Bronze Age industries and megalithic builders throughout Europe. Rapid expansion of Bell Beaker ceramics occurred around 2250–2000 B.C. Its origin appears to have been on the Iberian peninsula and graves of the period along the coasts of Portugal contained this type of pottery. Its use as grave goods, probably containing a last drink for the journey, was particularly pronounced in the valley of the Tejo, at Palmela, Sintra, Vila Nova de São Pedro, and at Alapraia.

Terra Sigillata

A red ware with a glossy surface, plain or decorated was first produced in Italy in the first century B.C., and later in southern and central Gaul in the first three centuries A.D. It was widely imitated and in Portugal as elsewhere, it is associated with sites of that period, generally Roman. The term *sigillata* derives from the stamp by which the potter signed his product.

Chronological Table

B.C.			
1,000,000	Lower Paleolithic		Homo erectus
100,00	Middle Paleolithic		Homo neanderthal
40,000	Upper Paleolithic		Homo sapiens
10,000	Mesolithic		
5,000	Neolithic		
4,000			Megalithic structures
3,500			
3,000		Chalcolithic	
2,500			
2,000	Bronze Age		
1,500			
1,000			
	Iron Age Celts	Phoenician, Greek and Punic influence	
750			
500			
250		Roman period	
0			
A.D.			
250			
500	Germanic period		
750	Arab period		
1,000		Christian reconquest	
1,250			

16. Chronological Table

The dates here are only approximate and are based on a composite of those given by various specialists in Portuguese early history. They are a general guide for the traveller in Portugal and must not be taken too literally. The identification of ancient cultures does not fit neatly into chronological slots. Among the stone and flint artifacts of a Mesolithic hunting camp may appear the bones of a domestic goat or sheep, or a polished stone tool characteristic of the later Neolithic period. A settled Neolithic community may display appropriate agricultural features such as production of cereals and the domestication of animals but have no pottery, only stone vessels—hallmarks of an earlier age. The collective set of distinctive features, then, that are employed to denote a chronological phase in human cultural evolution (Neolithic, Chalcolithic, Bronze Age) are seemingly not developed or transmitted all at once. Each feature is presumably accepted or rejected relative to the economic needs of the community. The overlapping and mutual exclusivity of cultural characteristics and geographical distribution is reflected in the fact that dates extend across various periods.

17. Conclusion

Out of the many and diverse cultures ranging over millennia that were imposed on a narrow strip of land along the western edge of the Iberian peninsula, a certain uniformity was moulded, given impetus under Roman law, administration and language, and later by a unified Christian ideal against Moslem communities.

By the end of the twelfth century in what became Portugal, the inhabitants were culturally and socially more homogeneous than the populations of many other areas of Europe. There were no ethnic subgroups of importance save the small Jewish community and a few remaining Moslems in the south of the country, nor were there any major regional groups devoted to their own autonomy. By the middle of the thirteenth century, Portugal had become the first nation-state in Europe. This early unification was important no doubt in preparing Portugal for its later role as the first western country to chart the world's oceans and open trade routes to new and distant lands.

PART TWO
SITES AND SIGHTS

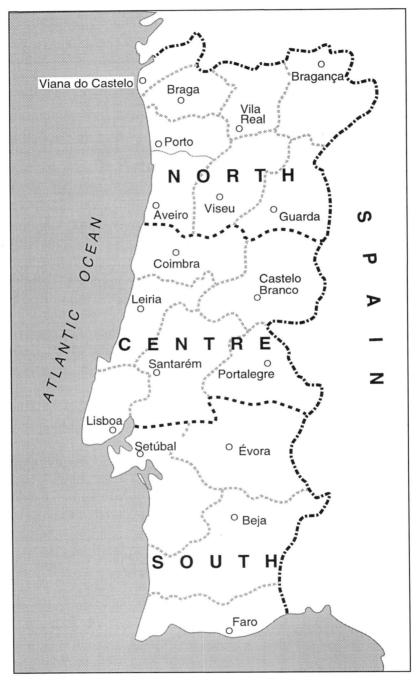

Map 5. District capitals

Administrative Districts

The ancient sites and sights of mainland Portugal are identified geographically within the eighteen administrative districts of the country, which are grouped here into three areas: north, central and south. They are presented in alphabetical order within each grouping.

The reader is generally directed to the various archaeological and historical sites from the capital city of each district.

Sources of Information, Conventions

In seeking local information concerning the whereabouts and condition of historical sites the following places offer assistance:

1. Turismo offices. Located in all major towns and cities and often in smaller places.

2. Câmara Municipal or Town Hall. Generally helpful and with a resident archaeologist and/or archaeological survey maps. The key to locked sites is generally here or at the local museum.

3. A local archaeological museum can be found in most towns and cities.

Many sites that are maintained by the Ministry of Culture are closed on Mondays.

While there are numerous maps of Portugal, the Michelin was most heavily relied upon by the authors.

Place names are given in Portuguese, e.g., Lisboa for Lisbon, Tejo for the Tagus river. This is the form encountered in the country and on most maps. Similarly, road signs to a site are given in the local language, e.g., *Ruinas Romanas* (Roman ruins) or *Anta de Arca* (Dolmen of Arca) in order to relate the guidebook to the roadside directions (if any).

Technical and local terms are kept to a minimum but useful references can be found in the glossary.

NORTHERN PORTUGAL

DISTRICTS

The districts of northern Portugal are: Aveiro, Braga, Bragança, Guarda, Porto (old name: Oporto), Viana do Castelo, Vila Real and Viseu. Bragança is the largest (and least populated) region and Viana do Castelo the smallest. The principal river, the Douro, flowing from east to west is fed by numerous tributaries. Other important rivers all feeding into the Atlantic Ocean are the Minho bordering Spain in the north, the Lima issuing into the Atlantic at Viana do Castelo, the Cávado exiting west of Braga at Esposende and the Vouga which enters the sea near Aveiro.

In the north the major mountain ranges of the Serra de Peneda and the Serra do Gerês constitute a large and rugged national park. No traces of Paleolithic man have yet been found in the park and it is assumed that human habitation in this sector of Portugal began only about five thousand B.C. along with the appearance of megalithic structures. The remains of the Roman road that linked Bracara Augusta (Braga) to Asturica Augusta (Astorga in Spain) over the Serra do Gerês along the river Homem, and the numerous milestones, are important traces of Roman military history in the area. The remains of the eleventh century castle at Castro Laboreiro stands as a Medieval sentinel in the mountains.

The northern sector of the country is characterized by hilly and mountainous terrain, an eastern plateau north of Guarda, and a coastal strip along the Atlantic ocean. The prehistory of the area is primarily characterized by numerous dolmens and castros. The castro that has the most to offer the visitor in terms of a large, well-maintained site is the Citânia de Briteiros. Running a close second is the Citânia de Sanfins, although the latter is less formal with no guardian/guide and with less diversity of sights. Its isolation, tranquility and sheer size, however, lend it a certain sublime charm.

The Romans were slow to subdue the northern mountains and valleys but they have left some spectacular remains such as the bridge at Chaves and the Roman town of Tongobriga (Freixo) at Marco de Canaveses.

Germanic Suevi found refuge in this relatively quiet corner of the Empire but were overthrown by the Visigoths. The most important legacies of the Visigothic period are the Igreja de São Frutuoso de Montélios on the outskirts of Braga and the basilica of São Pedro at Balsemão near Lamego.

The Moslems did not establish extensive settlements in the north of the country and have left only a few traces such as a ruined castle near Bragança.

Aveiro

The district of Aveiro now forms approximately the northern third of the old province of Beira Litoral. The capital, dating from Roman times, once lay directly on the sea but silt from the river Vouga eventually built up a spit of land off the coast leaving only a narrow channel to the sea. In more recent history, the channel has been closed and reopened by storms but the canal-crossed city remains an important port. The surrounding region, low-lying along the coast and hilly to the east, contains various dolmens (many unexcavated), such as those at Arouca, ancient Celtic settlements, for example at Lamas do Vouga and Roman and Medieval remains near Sever do Vouga.

Braga

Linked by important military roads to other parts of Lusitania, Roman Bracara Augusta became a major town and military headquarters for the northwestern section of the peninsula. With the demise of the Roman Empire the area fell under the dominion of the Suevi who held it for over a century and a half establishing Braga as the capital of their kingdom. It then passed into the hands of the Visigoths for another three hundred years until the town was taken by the Moslems in A.D. 715. Retaken by Christian forces under Don Alfonso, king of Oviedo, twenty-five years later, it was only subdued again by Moslem troops under al-Mansur, in 985. The Sé, or cathedral, of Braga was erected under the direction of Dom Henrique and DoñaTeresa in the twelfth century. The capital and its district form the southern half of the old province of Minho.

The area is well-endowed with ancient remains with the Fonte do Idolo, a national monument of, some say, pre-Roman vintage, an excavation of the Roman Colina de Maximinos, and the pre-Romanesque chapel of São Frutuoso within or near the capital. In the surrounding countryside are various megalithic sites, dolmens and menhirs, and Medieval anthropomorphic tombs, especially in the neighbourhood of Esposende. Castros abound, such as the famous Citânia de Briteiros and the Castro de São Lourenço at Vila Chã.

Bragança

Situated in the northeast corner of the country and surrounded by mountains, Bragança incorporates the eastern half of the old province of Tras-Os-Montes. (The western half is now Vila Real.) The capital, Bragança, Celto-Roman Iuliobriga, lies above the valley of the river Sabor at an altitude of 648 metres.

Above the town is situated the old castle, constructed in the twelfth century by king Sancho I but rebuilt in the fourteenth century. Within the walls of the castle is the Romanesque Domus Municipalis or Town Hall, a severe pentagonal granite structure of the twelfth century built over a Roman cistern. It is one of the few secular buildings of the period in Portugal. The surrounding region offers pre-Roman sites from rock paintings, e.g., at Mogadouro, to megalithic tombs, interesting Roman remains as at Vale de Telhas, and the old monastic ruins of Castro de Avelãs among others. The district was only sparsely settled in antiquity.

Guarda

The district now forms the eastern half of the old province of Beira Alta while Viseu makes up roughly the western half. The capital lies to the north-east of the Serra da Estrêla and is the country's highest city (about 1056 m). There was a fortified town here in Roman times. In 80 B.C. it sided with Sertorius, the Roman rebel, and later suffered attacks by Caesar's forces. The town was devastated by the Moslems and the inhabitants fled leaving their homes which soon became derelict. Only in the twelfth century did repopulation of the city begin under Sancho I. The city received its royal charter in 1199. Construction of the castle was begun in the twelfth century and the Ferreiros tower, part of the bulwarks of the town, also dates back to that period. While the city offers the visitor an historic Jewish quarter and the Romanesque church and excavation at Póvoa do Mileu, the environs contain rock paintings, pre-Roman megalithic tombs such as the dolmen near the village of Pêra do Moço, stretches of Roman roads, and the ancient inscriptions of Cabeço das Fráguas.

Porto (Oporto)

This northwest district corresponds to the old province of the Douro Litoral and the capital lies only 6 km from the mouth of the important river Douro. Porto is the second largest city after Lisboa. It lies on the north side of the river with Vila Nova de Gaia on the south side. The city's name dates back to pre-Roman Cale which became Portus Cale under the Romans. The Suevi and later the Visigoths had strongholds here but the town was taken by the Arabs in 716 and reconquered in 1092. Centuries of war depopulated the town. Henrique of Burgundy acquired the title of Duke of Portucalense in the eleventh century and the area later gave its name to the kingdom called Portugal. The countryside around Porto is rich in archaeological sites from rupestrian engravings at Penhafidelis, megalithic monuments near Penafiel, a menhir at Luzim, Iron Age castros, for example, at Monte Mozinho, Roman remains and Medieval tombs.

Viana do Castelo

Bordering Spain, this northwest district comprises the northern part of the old province of Minho with the capital, Viana do Castelo, at the mouth of the river Lima below Monte Luzia. Above the town and the mouth of the river is the castle which was constructed by Philip II. While the town was formed by a charter issued by King Afonso III in 1258, its remote ancestor may be the Celtic Citânia of Santa Luzia on the hill behind the city, later occupied by the Romans. Suevi and Visigoths occupied the town but left little behind in the form of tangible structures. It was conquered and occupied by the Moslems in the eighth and ninth centuries. In the region are prehistoric dolmens such as that of Bairrosa, near Vila Praia da Ancora and menhirs, castros and Medieval cemeteries. Roman bridges remain, as at Ponte de Lima and Rubiães.

Vila Real

The district forms what was once the western half of the old province of Tras-Os-Montes. Evidence of preCeltic peoples in the area is slight but Celts and Romans have left a good deal of their cultural features in evidence. During the Germanic invasions and that of the Moslems the region was generally depopulated. Not until the twelfth century did people begin to return to the area. There is much of archaeological interest here such as the dolmens at Alijó, Chã, and numerous other places, the Castro de Carvalhelos near Boticas, the Roman bridge and inscriptions over the river Tâmega at Chaves, the sanctuary at Panóias, and rock paintings at Carlão and Mairos.

Viseu

The capital is situated on the left bank of the river Paiva. The hill on which it stands is thought to have been inhabited by Celts, and on the northern outskirts are the remains of an unusual hexagonal Roman camp. The district now occupies roughly the western half of the old province of Beira Alta and lies in the very heart of the northern area nearly equidistant from the Atlantic seaboard and the borders of present-day Spain. Its geographical location has made it subject to numerous migrations of peoples from Paleolithic to modern times. In the vicinity are rupestrian paintings, for instance at Benfeitas, dolmens, as at Arca, important engraved stones at Serrazes and Lamas de Moledo, and castros such as that of Cárcoda near Carvalhais. Numerous stretches of Roman roads, bridges, and remains of spas still exist as may be seen around São Pedro do Sul on the river Vouga.

SITES AND SIGHTS

AVEIRO

Arouca

Forty-one antas or mamoas have been found in the parish of Escariz to the west of Arouca, distributed along a line less than 10 km long running northwest to south southeast. Many have been destroyed, but four in various stages of preservation have been excavated. Some exhibit painted or engraved decorative motifs. The dolmens, referred to as Portela de Antas, south of Arouca at Albergaria dos Cabras, and that of the Mamoa da Aliviada at Escariz are perhaps the best preserved. This latter has rupestrian paintings.

In the back outside wall of the church of Fermedo, west of Arouca near Escariz, is a marble stone with a Latin funerary inscription of about the first century.

Just outside the town toward the southwest at Igueiredo is a reputed Moslem tower in good condition with a cistern, loopholes and an undeciphered inscription. It stands among houses on private property.

Sights:

Dolmens (one with paintings), Latin funerary inscription and Moslem tower

Location:

Arouca lies NE of Aveiro. Take the EN 224 E off the N 1 at Oliveira de Azemeis and go ca. 30 km E to Arouca. Escariz is 13.5 km from Arouca. Go W 4.5 km to Rossas, then NW on the 326.

For the Moslem tower take the road back to Burgo and go S ca. 4 km to Igueiredo. Albergaria is on the same road further S.

Lamas do Vouga

Cabeço do Vouga, excavations here have revealed a rectangular enclosure of 34.65 m by 42.25 m whose walls stand as much as 3.3 m high. On the buttressed western side were four semicircular structures. Remains of these are located within the compound. Finds include Roman coins of the third and fourth centuries A.D. Little to see since the site is presently covered over but may again be opened.

Sights:
Luso-Roman fort currently covered over.

Location:
E of Averio on the N 1. At the village of Lamas go off the N 1 (ca. 6 km S of Agueda) and follow road back around under bridge (bridge on the N 1). Go past large house and take track right up to top of hill.

Rôge
The Igreja Matriz de Rôge has an anthropomorphic stone coffin beside it. There is also a stone embedded in the wall inside the church engraved with the date of 1107. The baptismal font has a Medieval base. There is a Roman bridge nearby at Castelo.

Sights:
Anthropomorphic coffin, engraved stone, baptismal font, Roman bridge.

Location:
NE of Aveiro. Go off the EN 1 at Oliveira de Azeméis and E on the EN 224 ca. 11 km (bad, cobblestone road) to Vale de Cambra. Go through town on main street and follow road uphill (signposted *São Pedro do Sul*) to Rôge. Church in village. For the bridge, continue down through village to the bottom of the hill and ask for the Ponte Romana do Castelo.

Other sites and sights in the district of Aveiro include:

Sever do Vouga
NE of Aveiro on the N 328. The Anta da Cerqueira, is a dolmen NE of Sever do Vouga in the Serra da Gralheira on the N328-1. Also in the

Anthropomorphic coffin, Rôge

vicinity is the Pedra Insculturada, Forno dos Mouros (guide recommended as it is of very difficult access), and monolithic structures at Talhadas W of Aveiro on the E 80 just before the border of Viseu.

BRAGA

Barcelos
Castro de Carvalhal (Franqueira). Pre-Roman settlement on the left bank of the Cávado river. Small but fairly well-preserved site. Ten or so round houses

and several rectangular ones make up the dwellings, some with antechambers. Steps lead up to a higher precinct. Two large natural rocks sentinel the entrance to the second enclosure. Easy access, unfenced. Besides the natural defensive hilltop, the site is surrounded by a stout wall close to the base of the hill enclosing houses, and a second wall surrounds the summit, defining a fairly small enclosure. The site is known locally as O Castelo.

Sights:
Castro with round and square house remains, steps, walls.

Location:
Barcelos is W of Braga on the N 103. Just before entering town, follow signs for Póvoa de Varzim. Ca. 1 km turn left at sign for Cavalhal/Franqueira. Follow this (poor) road 4.3 km from turnoff and shortly after passing a round stone tower on left, some steps appear and almost immediately on the right is a path. Follow this ca. 25 m and the site is on the right. Alternatively, drive to church at top of hill, 5.4 km from turnoff, and walk down steps to road below, then go left and the path is on the right.

Braga
Abutting the eighteenth century church of São Francisco is the tiny Visigothic chapel of São Frutuoso de Montélios founded in the seventh century by Frutuoso de Dume, Bishop of Braga. Said to be one of the oldest churches in Portugal, it shows Byzantine influence which is rare in this country.

Built on a Greek cross plan with a reconstructed

Castro de Carvalhal (Franqueira), Barcelos

central dome, the chapel may be reached by steps from inside the church of São Francisco. The vaults are supported by marble columns and an ornamental frieze is preserved but the entire structure was remodelled in the eleventh century and has been somewhat restored in more recent times. The exterior displays blind arcades and is surrounded by decorative bands of marble.

The excavation of the Roman city of Bracara, Colina de Maximinos, begun in earnest in 1977, is currently in progress and several necropoli have been found in the vicinity. The results of continuing excavations have so far unearthed an extensive thermal and drainage system, tiled dwellings and walls. Behind stout stone walls the excavation is currently closed to the public but the gate is open when work is in progress. A museum is planned at the site. For more information contact Campo Arqueologico da Universidade do Minho.

Fonte do Idolo, a spring and sanctuary of Roman or pre-Roman times consists of a figure in a toga and a female bust engraved in the rock.

Sights:

Seventh century Visigothic chapel, excavation of the Roman city and an ancient spring and sanctuary.

Fonte do Idolo, Braga

Locations:

All the sites are either centrally located or in the suburbs of the town. São Frutuoso is reached by taking the road out of town marked Ponte de Lima ca. 3 km. Here, there is a sign on the right for the church. Go right and follow stone crosses. The church abuts the larger one and has a guardian/guide.

The excavations are on the Avenida de Imaculada Conceição on the edge of town and the Fonte do Idolo is off the Avenida de la Liberdade beside the Casa de Saúde, through an iron gate and down some steps. The Turismo Office will provide maps for all these sights.

Briteiros

The remains of the Iron Age settlement of Citânia de Briteiros were discovered in the late nineteenth century with excavations beginning in 1875. It is reputed to have flourished during the fourth and third centuries B.C. Romans also occupied this site which consists of a settlement enclosed within three rings of walls containing some one hundred-and-fifty round, oval or rectangular, mostly single-roomed, dwellings. The streets are paved with slabs of stone. Two of the round dwellings have been reconstructed on the model of the *trulli* of Apulia or the Sardinian *nuraghi*, on the theory that a circular dwelling with a conical roof was the basic type of human habitation. There remains some doubt about the authenticity of the reconstruction.

Visigothic chapel of São Frutuoso, Braga

The cultural life at Briteiros lasted down to the Barbarian invasions. The latest coin of a Roman emperor found at Briteiros is of Constantine the Great (A.D. 306-337).

There is a good view of the excavations from the chapel of São Romão on top of the hill. The site is fenced and open during normal hours. It is unusual among castros north of the Douro in having its houses arranged along streets in a grid pattern.

Downhill, beside a monument alongside the road leading toward Guimarães, is what appear to have been baths and the water conduit running down into them is still

Citânia de Briteiros, partial view

clearly visible. Of interest also are the cisterns and the ancient fountain from whence the water issued forth from the rock. On the summit of the hill are the remains of a necropolis.

Close by, just north of Taipas is the Castro de Sabroso, another smaller hill-top fort surrounded by a huge wall of dressed stone but with only a little over thirty, mostly circular houses. This site is smaller and older than Briteiros and was probably abandoned earlier. The existence of coins and stamped Roman pottery—Terra Sigillata—at these sites shows that they were in use in Roman times.

Fragments of pottery (much of it painted), carved stones, weapons, implements and jewelry recovered during excavations are now in the Museu de Martins Sarmento in Guimarães.

Sights:
Large excavated site of Citânia de Briteiros with defensive walls, dwellings, paved streets, cisterns, fountain, water conduits, baths, reconstructed dwellings, remains of necropolis and small museum.

Castro de Sabroso has a single, large wall with thirty-five circular and three rectangular houses.

Location:
The Citânia de Briteiros is located ca. 7.5 km N of Guimarães and 12 km E of Braga on Monte São Romão in the hills of the Serra Falperra. Take the road between Braga and Guimarães to Taipas (9 km Guimarães, 16 km Braga). Turn off E at sign for *Citânia/Póvoa de Lanhosa*. Follow sign for *Citânia* 4.6 km and at São Estavão de Briteiros go 4 km to left at sign. Well signposted at top of hill. Site can also be reached from Braga via Bomjesús.

Sabroso can be reached from Taipas by the road toward Santa Christina de Longos. After ca. 2.5 km turn right at Cancela and go 278 m to the top. From Taipas, it is 4 km.

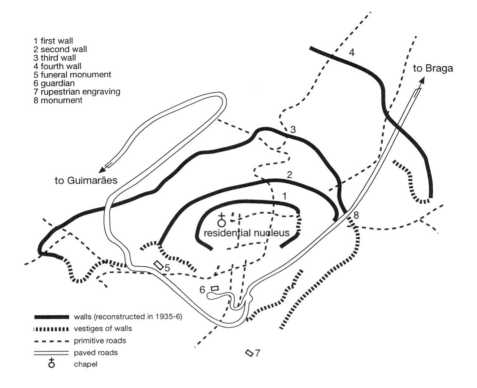

1 first wall
2 second wall
3 third wall
4 fourth wall
5 funeral monument
6 guardian
7 rupestrian engraving
8 monument

to Braga

to Guimarães

residential nucleus

walls (reconstructed in 1935-6)
vestiges of walls
primitive roads
paved roads
chapel

*Plan of the Defensive Organization of the Citânia de Briteiros
(after Mario Cardozo)*

Esposende

The Medieval necropolis of nearly 200 excavated graves, and more unexcavated, is one of the largest in the Iberian peninsula. The site, near the sea, was covered over by the advancing sand dunes. Walls of a house within the cemetery, perhaps that of the caretaker, have been uncovered. In some of the graves are the stones employed to support the head in a fixed position facing east toward Jerusalem in order to view the second coming of Christ. At the time of writing there was at least one covered grave with a skeleton still inside.

In the vicinity of Esposende are several menhirs including one at São Bartolomeu do Mar, 2.10 m high, a few metres from the church of that name and another at São Paio de Antas, 1.65 m high.

Near Vila Chã are three dolmens, but only one (minus the capstone but with engravings) has been excavated. Other mamoas, some partially uncovered, are clearly visible.

In the Parish of Vila Chã stands the hill called O Monte da Cerca (or da Maceira) the highest point in the area, a climb of about 250 m to the top. The summit is crowned by some massive, roughly hewn granite blocks that form the remains of an ancient wall whose chronology remains elusive. Forty metres to the north are the remains of a megalithic tomb constituting the burial chamber and the entrance corridor but still covered in part by the mamoa.

The so-called Mamoa da Portelagem is situated near Abelheira in the extreme west of the parish and consists of the roofless burial chamber of a dolmen under excavation.

At Terroso in the parish of Palmeira de Faro are located the Iron Age site of Castro do Senhor dos Desamparados and the vestiges of a proto-historic necropolis at the Quinta de Mereces or Cimo de Vila (little to see). Near the necropolis, by the wall around the property, is one of the most important dolmens in the area. It is large size and in spite of successive pillaging, preserves four supports of the grand chamber, two of which display original engravings.

Also near Vila Chã are the remains of the Castro de São Lourenço. This Iron Age site is situated on various terraced levels with steps near the summit of a hill and was defended by two stone walls reinforced on the eastern side by earthworks. On the top of the hill now stands a chapel dedicated to São Lourenço. Romanization of the site is clear from ceramic finds, silver Roman coins and an altar dedicated to Dea Sancta among other things. The castro appears to have been occupied until at least the fourth century A.D. This is an ongoing excavation of difficult access displaying remains of circular and rectangular houses., steps, millstones and some parts of walls (there were three).

The Iron Age Castro de Belinho at São Pão de Antas located on a small hill above the Quinta de Belinho was partially excavated in the twenties. It was protected by three walls on two sides and contains various stone foundations of mostly circular dwellings and cattle enclosures now covered by foliage. One rectangular foundation suggests Romanization of the site.

In the northeast corner of the churchyard in Forjães may be seen a Medieval stone-covered coffin and at Eira d'Ana is a Medieval anthropomorphic style grave cut from the living rock, the only one of its kind in the district of Esposende. It is now behind the walls of a private residence. Its location, however, was once beside the well-travelled road from Esposende to Barcelos. Such graves, reminders of the frailty of life, frequently called passers-by to prayer.

Sights:

Medieval necropolis. Menhirs. Dolmens. Castros.

Castro de São Lourenço, Vila Chã, Esposende

Location:

Esposende is situated on the coast due W of Braga.

The Medieval necropolis is in Fão, 3 km S of Esposende. Cross the bridge over the river Cávado, take first right then short left and right again on Rua das

Covales. Go to T junction and turn right. Excavation is on the left in open ground amidst urban development with railway on one side. There is a sign *Campo Arqueológico* at the partially covered site. The gate may be locked and it is best to inquire first at the Turismo office or the Câmara Municipal in Esposende.

The menhir easiest to find is at São Bartolomeu do Mar in a field behind the church and behind a wall. Go N of Esposende along the coast on the E 01/N13 for 5 km and turn in left at church with blue tiles on the façade. For the other menhirs in Antas and Forjães, the Turismo Office in Esposende will help with maps.

For Vila Chã, continue on road toward Viana from Esposende and turn off right to Saõ Pão de Antas. Upon reaching the cemetery, take right fork toward Vila Chã. Continue 2.5 km and dolmen is on the right. From the football field in Vila Chã go 900 m on Vila Chã-Antas road (S) and there is a dolmen on the left.

After the football field turn right off the main road in the direction of Abelheira. Go 700 m to fork. Walk up left fork 200-300 m and go left at next fork. Walk down to wall on the right and a dolmen with a capstone is in the corner of the field.

The chapel of São Lourenço can be seen to the E from the main road toward Viana and, along with the castro, is 3.6 km from Esposende. Once you arrive at the chapel, take the path to the right going down toward the sea and you will come to the castro.

Medieval necropolis, Fão, Esposende

Galegos Santa Maria

There are baths, perhaps Roman, in the middle of an apparent castro. Not unlike the baths at Briteiros, this unusual structure consists of a grotto in a wall of rock and two arches forming an entranceway. Designs appear on some of the stone work as, for example, the upright slab of stone on the right on the face of the first arch.

Sights:
Possible Roman bath or perhaps pre-Roman.

Location:
W of Braga. From Barcelos cemetery take the N 205 toward Prado. Go 3.7 km to sign for Galegos Santa Maria, left. Follow the road but do not go left at sign *Termas*. Instead, pass through next small village. Turn left at church proceeding up hill. At fork go right, sign *Escola.*. Go past the school on the right

and fork left. Go to T and then left up narrow, rutted dirt road. At the next fork go left. Park by last house (where ceramics are made). Walk up path to right near house and site is a few metres along, fenced but gate unlocked. From the sign to Galegos on the main road to the school is ca. 2 km. From the school to the site is 700 m. Information can be gained at the school if you are lost!

Guimarães

On the lower slope of the Penha is the former monastery of Santa Marinha da Costa of which the oldest written reference dates back to 959. The structure was entirely rebuilt in the eighteenth century and is now a Pousada. Excavations have revealed the existence of a small Roman tower, traces of a Visigothic basilica and remains of a Moslem building. Still in place is an Arabic doorway at the base of what was once a tower and which is considered

Ancient baths, Galegos Santa Maria

one of the finest pieces of Arabic architecture in the country. There is also a Medieval anthropomorphic tomb in the courtyard.

Above the town is the castle with a tenth century keep and high slender battlements. One of the most complete and best-preserved Medieval strongholds in Portugal, it was the birthplace of the first Portuguese king, Afonso Henriques. Below the castle entrance stands the small chapel of São Miguel of 1105 where Afonso Henriques was baptized.

Sights:

Arabic and Medieval remains in Pousada of Santa Marinha and tenth century castle.

Location:

Guimarães is 24 km SE of Braga on N 101. The Pousada and castle are signposted in town.

Ponte São Vicente

Citânia of São Julião. Fortified hilltop town occupied during the Late Bronze Age. The oldest defenses consisted of an earthen wall and a ditch or moat protecting the circular style stone huts, and date back to the ninth century B.C.

The site was occupied by Iron Age peoples and was eventually Romanized. There are later remains of rectangular dwellings, walls, streets and remnants of three protecting walls. It lies on top and along the slope of a steep hill on the right bank of the river Homem. Only certain sections have been excavated. On the summit of the hill is a small chapel.

The remains around the chapel are from the Iron Age and those below date back to the Bronze Age. There are seemingly three groups of habitation spilling down the mountainside. Open site.

Sights:

Fortified hilltop town with excavations revealing Iron and Bronze Age structures.

Location:

N of Braga and NE of Vila Verde. Leave Vila Verde on road toward Caldelas. Pass the turnoff, right, for Caldelas and follow signs for Ponte São Vicente (village itself is not signposted, but from the Caldelas turnoff is 1.9 km to a church on the right). Turn left opposite church onto narrow street and follow this. At triple fork take right 700 m to a 160 degree turn (left) onto dirt road. Proceed 800 m to chapel at top of steep, rutted road. Excavations on route and around and below chapel.

Citânia de São Julião, Ponte São Vicente

Póvoa de Lanhosa

Small excavation of a Roman site. There is a twelfth century castle on the hill above the town but the Roman site is in a modern urban area. It was discovered recently when digging the foundations of a new house. The remains are ca. 2 m below the surface of the ground and consist of remnants of dwellings and walls. The latter appear to extend well beyond the property and the entire hill of the current development may once have been occupied. There is little to see at present.

Sights:

Slight excavation of Roman site and twelfth century castle.

Location:

Póvoa de Lanhosa is located E of Braga 19 km off the N 103. Entering town on the Taipas-Guimarães road, go left at the crossroads signposted Braga-Chaves. After 600 m turn left at sign for Lanhosa. Go up the hill 900 m and turn left at sign *Cim de Vila/Tinoces*. Turn right ca. 15 m and on the right, between modern houses, is the site.

Sabroso

Castro de Sabroso. See Briteiros.

Other sites and sights in the district of Braga include:

Caldas das Taipas

Roman bridge on the N 101 between Braga and Guimarães at the junction with the N 310.

Celorico de Basto

Partially restored castle of perhaps the eleventh century. SE of Braga on N 101 to Amarante, then NE on N 210, 23 km. Near the Vila Real border.

Valdozende

Three-arched Roman bridge. NE of Braga and near the Peneda-Gerês park at Terras de Bouro.

Vila Nova de Famalicão

There are some remnants of Iron Age defensive hilltop settlements in the area such as the Castro das Emidas near Jesufrei and the Castro de S. Miguel-o-Anjo near Calendario. There are also reputed milestones according to some maps but the authors were unable to locate them The town is south of Braga about 25 km and a little beyond Gavião off the N 14.

Vila Verde

The nearby Castro do Barbuda at Monte Castelo displays little to see having been covered over for protection. There are plans to reopen the site for further excavation. N of Braga and W of Vila Verde on road to Laje. Go 1.3 km to church on right and turn in there. Follow cobblestone road up to top 1.5 km. At top, walk up to site.

BRAGANÇA

Bragança

The ancient granite boar by the castle gate serves as a base for a pillory. The original construction of the castle, with well preserved walls and keep, dates back to the twelfth century as does the City Hall.

The Castro de Sacóias has little left to see although quoted in guides to the area. It was located on a hill to the right of a chapel above the village of Sacóias, but is now a vineyard littered with ceramics and slate from the ancient site.

The Castro de Avelãs has few remains. There is a rebuilt monastery in the village from the twelfth century which is now mostly in ruins. It is unique in Portugal as the only one constructed of brick with blind arcades in the style of those at Sahagún in Spain. Remains of old walls, reputedly dating back to the seventh century, and part of the entranceway remain. Note there are many towns with the name of "Castro" where the original castro has long since disappeared.

Sights:

Ancient stone boar, ruined Medieval monastery.

Locations:

The boar is in town inside the castle gate.

Sacóias is located NE of Bragança on the N 218-1 toward Rio de Onor. Take N 218 from Bragança E and turn left (N) on 218-1. Turn right at Sacóias and go to the bottom of the village by the water trough. Turn left and follow the road to T junction. Turn right to top of hill to chapel. There are reputed early graves at the chapel, but they seem to have disappeared.

Avelãs is W of Bragança. Leaving town on the road toward Chaves turn left immediately after the overhead railway bridge. After 2.6 km turn right at sign for *Castro* and *Mosteiro.* Monastery is in village.

Carrazeda de Ansiães

Beside the church of São João Baptista Extra Muros (outside the walls), on the south side, are three anthropomorphic rock-cut tombs.

Sights:

Three Medieval rock-cut tombs.

Location:

Carrazeda de Ansiães is SW of Bragança near the Viseu border. Go 66 km to Mirandela, then S on the N 213/N 214 ca. 40 km. (See also, entries for Vilarinho da Castanheira, Zedes.)

Mazouco

In 1982 a group of three zoomorphic Paleolithic engravings in the living rock was discovered near Mazouco beside the river Douro. The most complete and spectacular is that of a horse about 62 cm in length by 37.5 cm in height. It appears to date back to about 13,000-10,000 B.C. Local legend says the horse is looking at the river to where a treasure is buried.

Paleolithic rock engraving, Mazouco

Sight:

Paleolithic engravings.

Location:

Go SE of Bragança on the N 218/N 221 to near the Spanish border. It is just N of Freixo de Espada Cinta. Take the road E into Mazouco and pass through the village and almond orchards following the road down toward the river. (Many hairpin bends.) At fork go left and at second fork (three pathways) take the central one ca. 500 m. Then walk down narrow path toward river for about another 500 m (one might also wish to leave the car at the trifurcation). The rock is on the left at the bottom of the path facing the river. It may take a little searching around. Someone in the village will act as guide.

Mogadouro

Penas Róias, with its ruins of a Medieval castle and tower, is also the site of Fraga da Letra, Bronze Age paintings on the side of a small grotto on a rocky promontory topped by the remains of a castro. Of the castro there is now little left to see. There is also a stone sculptured boar near the church at Vila dos Sinos.

Sights:

Bronze Age paintings. Remains of a castro. Stone boar.

Location:

Mogadouro is due S of Bragança some 80 km. For the Bronze Age paintings take the N 219 road NE out of Mogadouro toward Azinhoso. Go 7.6 km and turn right at sign for Penas Róias. Drive to top of town and castle (O castelo). The paintings are on the left side of the hill facing it from the

Bronze Age paintings, Fraga de Letra, Mogadouro

village but they are not easy to find. If in doubt ask locals for Fraga da Letra.

Vila dos Sinos is S of Bragança and E of Mogadouro ca. 8 km on the N 221 to Santiago, then S on road to Vilarinho dos Galegos. The village is before Vilarinho.

Vale de Telhas

The town contains a fountain of Roman origin, a military column beside the fountain and another beside the school on entering town, a wine press cut into the living stone with a hole into a lower basin for the collection of liquid. Three houses in the village have Roman stones in the walls, one with a Latin inscription, another with Early Christian symbols and a defensive window. There is a nearby bridge which may be Roman, and just outside the village several hundred metres along a farm road is a Roman vaulted structure over the natural spring with steps leading down into it. About 500 m away on a hillock are many small wine or oil pressing hollows cut in the rocks, grooves to funnel off the liquid, millstones and other artifacts.

Sights:

Roman fountain, military column, wine and oil presses, stones with inscription and Early Christian symbols, spring and millstones.

Location:

The village is SW of Bragança on the N 103, 73 km then ca. 6 km S on the N 315 and all sights are in or around the village. Much of the population turned out to help us identify the sights as they are very proud of their ancient remains.

Vilarinho da Castanheira

Megalithic tomb with some faded paintings and a nearby Roman bridge.

Sights:

Dolmen and Roman bridge.

Location:

The dolmen is near the village which is SW of Bragança near the borders of Viseu and Guarda. Coming on the N 213 S of Mirandela, go left (S) off the EN 214 just after Carvalho de Egas toward Vilarinho. The dolmen is situated off the EN 324 toward Cabeça but ask for directions in Vilarinho. The Roman bridge is just past Vilarinho on the EN 324.

House façade, Vale de Telhas

Anta de Zeda, Zedes

Zedes

Dolmen de Zedes. Nice specimen with half-a-dozen standing chamber stones and capstone in place. There is, however, little left of the passageway.

Sights:

Dolmen.

Location:

SW of Bragança and S of Mirandela. Take the EN 214 from Vila Flor (S of Macedo) toward Carrazeda de Ansiães. 1.6 km before reaching the town, turn right (N) toward Zedes. After the turnoff to Folgares, continue 1 km toward Zedes and the sign *Anta* is on the left. Dolmen can be seen from the road.

Other sites and sights in the district of Bragança include:

Abreiro

Small town near the river Tua in the northeast part of the country. Remains of Roman bridge. SW of Bragança and 14.5 km SW of Mirandela on the N 15 to just past Lamas de Oreilho, then S 11 km to Abreiro.

Duas Igrejas

Rock shelter with Late Paleolithic engravings located by going SE of Branganza to Miranda do Douro, then SW on the N 221 8 km to Duas Igrejas. 3 km S of this is the site. (Near the Spanish border.) Guide recommended.

Mirandela

Long Medieval bridge of seventeen arches over the Rio Tua, probably on Roman foundations. SW of Branganza ca. 66 km on the N 15/E 82.

Rebordãos

Remains of walls of a Moslem castle but not much left to see. SW of Bragança on the N 15 toward Mirandela ca. 10 km. Ask in village for the Castelo de Rebordãos about 3 km away.

Torre de Dona Chama

Ponte de Pedra, reconstructed Roman bridge SW of Bragança and NE of Mirandela on the N 206.

GUARDA

Almendra

Castelo Calabre is a Romanized hilltop fort that was occupied up to the Middle Ages. There is, however, little to see apart from the remains of the walls surrounding the site. Recommended for those who like to hike. Enjoy an excellent view at the end.

Sight:

Remains of castro walls.

Location:

Almendra is reached by going N of Guarda 84 km to Vila Nova da Fozcóa, then SE 17 km on the N 222. Leaving Almendra, take right turn toward Estação de Almendra. Pass through the terraced hills and almond groves 8.6 km. Turn left at sign for Quinta da Torrão and proceed up dirt track ca. 650 m to small stone house. Walk up to the top of larger hill on left. About one hour's walk.

Figueira de Castelo Rodrigo

Next to Nossa Senhora da Marofa sanctuary is a Roman inscription.

Nearby is the Roman temple, Casarão da Torre. The foundations are of an imposing Roman temple which preserves the podium and part of the upward structure. The building appears to have been used long after Roman times and was somewhat rebuilt in the sixteenth and seventeenth centuries. Excavations around the site have revealed bases of columns, stone floors, millstone and part of what may have been a tomb. Ca. 12 m high at its highest point, it is 10 m long and 7.5 m wide.

Sights:
Roman inscription, Roman temple remains and excavation.

Casarão da Torre, Roman temple, Figueira de Castelo Rodrigo

Location:
N of Guarda on N 221. The inscription is 3 km S of Figueira de Castelo Rodrigo off the N 221.

To reach Casarão da Torre take secondary road from town past the 13th century Cistercian convent of Sta. Maria de Aguiar to turn-off for Almofala (6.4 km from town). Take the left turn to Almofala and 2.6 km further on is a dirt farm track leading to the Roman structure that can be seen from the main road. The track is rough and overgrown but passable up to the site.

Fornos de Algodres
Two dolmens, the first has eight-and-one-half standing stones and the capstone is in place. One standing stone has been repaired and there is no passageway. The second is smaller than this one.

There is a possible Roman bridge and road further on at Matança, and about twenty Medieval rock-cut tombs in individual outcroppings of rock ca. 2 km beyond this.

Sights:
Dolmens. Roman bridge. Medieval tombs.

Location:
Fornos de Algodres is NW of Guarda on the N 16/E 80. Go N from here on the secondary road toward Matança. After ca. 7 km a blue sign, left (facing the wrong way) points to the dolmen. Turn in on gravel road and travel 400 m. The second dolmen is found by continuing on the Matança road ca. 500 m to a track on the right and following it for ca. 2 km.

What appears to be a Roman bridge and bit of road are in town and 2 km beyond Matança lies the tiny village of Forcadas. At the entrance to the village, on the left, are some white rocks in front of a small house with a red roof. In these rocks are the tombs. (Ask for cemeterio romano.)

Guarda

Póvoa do Mileu, remains of a Roman villa situated next to the eleventh century Romanesque church of Senhora do Mileu. The area excavated so far is rather small but reveals remains of baths, the hypocaust, water conduits, foundations of buildings, and fragments of columns. Some of the site was destroyed by the construction of the road into Guarda in 1951 when the remains were discovered. Artifacts from the pre-Roman Lusitanian Iron Age have also been found here.

Guarda has an old Judiaria or Jewish quarter one house of which, on the Rua don Sancho, the shop of a keymaker, displays an inscription.

Rock-cut tombs, Fornos de Algodres

Sights:

Remains of a Roman villa with baths, hypocaust, water conduits, column fragments, foundations. Judiaria.

Location:

The Roman ruins are located at the entrance to the town coming from the north. They are signposted *Ruinas Romanas de Póvoa do Mileu*. The Jewish quarter is signposted in town.

João Antão

An inscription engraved in the rock, Cabeço das Fráguas, in the Celtic language and the Latin alphabet, written probably in the second century A.D. The text refers to several deities to whom some animals were apparently sacrificed and has linguistic characteristics in common with the inscription of Lamas de Moledo. (See Lamas below.)

Sight:

Celtic rupestrian inscription.

Location:

Go SE of Guarda on the N 233 to Sortelhão, then SW to João Antão. From here take the narrow and poor mountain road toward Bendada. After ca. 4 km you can see the mountain top to the east. Leave the car and walk approximately 2 km across large granite rocks to a small plateau. The inscription is just below the top.

Pêra do Moço

Dolmen with five standing stones and capstone.

Sight:
Dolmen.

Location:
Ca. 16 km NE of Guarda. Take the EN 221 out of Guarda and pass Pêra do Moço and the turnoff W for Matrianes. A little further on, the dolmen can be seen on the right, 50 m from the road, in the middle of a field.

Cabeço das Fráguas near João Antão.
Courtesy J. Untermann

Other sites and sights in the district of Guarda include:

Folgosinho

Roman road. W of Guarda in the Serra da Estrêla, approached off the N 17 via Gouveia. Enquire in town for the *calzada romana.*.

PORTO

Alvarelhos

Castro de Alvarelhos. Ongoing excavation although very little to see at time of writing. Small area of digging revealed a few metres of stone structures.

Sight:
Scant remains of castro.

Location:
N of Porto, the site is not easy to find. Leave Santo Tirso on the road to Vila do Conde. Go 9 km to Trofa and at lights turn left toward Porto. After 4.4 km turn right to Alvarelhos. Go down in the village to the church, turn left and follow the road to a private entryway, right, which is lined with cement posts. This leads to the Quinta Paiço. Go up narrow road to top. Castro is here on private property and signposted as a national monument.

Baião

Eight dolmens all in poor and deteriorating condition. Passageways are discernible in some and a few seem to have more than one. All are beside the road and some are enclosed behind rusting, dilapidated fences. A strange, evocative corridor of megaliths.

Sights:
Remains of dolmens.

Location:
Baião is E of Porto and S of Amarante 15 km on the N 101, then W 10 km on the N 321. Pass through town (W) and turn right at sign for Marco. There is also a blue and gold sign indicating dolmens (but it's the first and last one). Drive 1.8 km and turn right on gravel road (sign for dolmens here destroyed). Continue for 1.6 km to fork and turn right. After 900 m stands a lone dolmen, now only scattered stones and a hole in the mamoa.

Ca. 600 m further on is Outeiro de Gregos which consists of four dolmens behind broken-down fences of which number 3 (the first on the right), is in the best condition with three standing stones. Ca. 500 m beyond this group is the Outeiro de Anta consisting of three dolmens. One is fenced. Two have three standing stones. (See also, entry for Ovil.)

Marco de Canaveses
Freixo (Roman Tongobriga). Large excavation of Roman town part of which is in the upper village but most down below. Excavations begun in 1980 have revealed baths constructed in the first century A.D. and used up until the fifth century. Walls more than five metres high and vaulted ceilings are still preserved. Besides the frigidarium, the buildings so far uncovered contained an open-air swimming pool with a surrounding arcade. A small bath was discovered next to the Roman baths in the pre-Roman style. Also found were cisterns, various altars, milestones, dwellings and numerous artifacts. The cemetery has been traced and soundings have revealed the locations of pre-Roman circular houses. Excavations are in progress with much more to be done.

Sights:
Large ongoing excavation of Roman Tongobriga including walls, milestones, dwellings, baths, cistern, pool, forum and altars.

Excavations, Freixo, Marco de Canaveses

Location:
Marco de Canaveses is E of Porto. Go to Penafiel and then SE 13 km on the N 15/N211 to Marco. Continue S on this road and sign on right points to *Ruinas Romanas 1000 m*. One excavation is found on top of the hill in the village. For the others, pass through the village and down the hill. Excavations are on left of road and more extensively a little further on to the right.

Monte Córdova

Monte do Padrão. A considerably Romanized hill-fort in which can be seen the remains of houses, a fountain, water conduits, a courtyard and streets. At one end of the Roman site appears to have been the original castro with circular houses. The area is only partially excavated. Also on top of the same hill, a short distance away, are the remains of a Medieval village with remnants of dwellings and tombs. About a hundred metres from the site in the chapel of Senhor do Padrão is part of an inscription.

Sights:

Roman ruins with houses, fountain, water conduits, walls and streets. Nearby Medieval village containing remnants of dwellings and some tombs. Inscription.

Location:

NE of Porto. Take the road from Santo Tirso toward Paços de Ferreira (see also entry for Sanfins). After 6.7 km from the turnoff at Santo Tirso, there is a sign in a small village reading *Estação Arqueológico de Monte Padrão*. Follow the road to the right and onto a path further down on right. At fork in path by wall take the left and go up badly rutted road to small church. The sites are on the hill to the right behind the church.

Ovil

Dolmen de Chã da Parada. Potentially a good specimen but the burial chamber is filled with dirt and the passageway has nearly disappeared. Large, heavy capstone is supposed to have engravings but they seem to have faded away.

Dolmen de Chã da Parada, Ovil

Sight:

Dolmen.

Location:

Ovil is E of Porto. Go S of Amarante on the N 101 then W on the N321 toward Baião. Coming from Baião toward Ovil (going E) after sign for Queimado, go over bridge and turn off at first road to the left. Continue up the same (gravel) road (do not go right) 1.7 km more (3 km from main road). Dolmen is on the right ca. 50 m off the road.

The dolmen is actually on the same road as those listed under Baião and could be reached by continuing E from there after passing the small church.

Penafiel

Nearby, in the vicinity of Oldrões lies Monte Mozinho and the Cidade Morta or Dead City. Here are the remains of a large fortified settlement. The site was occupied up to the fifth century A.D. The houses, built of stone, once had plastered and painted internal walls. Groups of dwellings, circular and rectangular, which often opened onto a paved courtyard, were each protected by low walls. Before the end of its life, the town had spilled out beyond the stout ramparts that enclosed it. Its apparent prosperity was probably due to the proximity of the gold mines in the nearby Serra das Banjas. Of the various castros in the area, this one stands out.

The menhir of Luzim in the parish of the same name stands 2.5 m high and appears to date back to the second millennium B.C. About 10 m to the E there is a petroglyph called Pegadinhas de São Gonçalo (St. Gonçalo's little footsteps) consisting of niches hewn from the stone. There is also the rupestrian engraving of Lomar in the vicinity.

At Boelhe stands the smallest Romanesque church in Portugal, that of São Gens, built in the twelfth century and now a national monument.

Also near Penafiel stands the Portela Dolmen of Santa Marta known as the Moor's Oven in the parish of Santa Marta with eight standing stones and a large capstone. Proto-Christian anthropomorphic tombs constructed in the living rock during the first half of the first millennium A.D. are located very near this dolmen.

In Penhafidelis there is a petroglyph which depicts a Lusitanian warrior dressed in a long tunic or sago, holding a short dagger in his right hand and a small round shield in the left. The outline of the figure is difficult to locate and a guide is recommended.

Anthropomorphic tombs can also be found at the Church of Cabeça Santa and the Chapel of Santa Catarina in Quintã, Peroselo, and in the courtyard of the twelfth century Romanesque Church of São Salvador de Gandra. Above the confluence of the rivers Douro and Tâmega near the town of Entre-os-Rios stood a castro whose remains now are difficult to discern.

(See also, São Vicente do Pinheiro.)

Sights:

Large Iron Age fortified settlement remains, menhir, dolmen, anthropomorphic tombs, twelfth century church with tombs, petroglyphs.

Portela dolmen of Santa Marta, Penafiel

Locations:

Penafiel lies 37 km E of Porto on the E 82/N 15. Oldrões is S of Penafiel. From the Turismo office in Penafiel go S 7.3 km on the EN 106. Turn right where there is a modern church on the left and a café on the right, and follow the road up the hill 1.5 km. Then turn right again onto a cobblestone roadway and proceed uphill 2 km. A rusted sign on the right beside a house reads *Mozinho*. Follow the dirt path 300 m and take right fork. Go 500 m further and castro is visible on the right.

The menhir and Pegadinhas de São Gonzalo petroglyph are at Luzim which is S of Penafiel on the N 320/312. Boelhe is further S on the N 312.

For the Portela Dolmen go to Santa Marta 2 km E of Penafiel on the road toward Vila Real, the N 15. In the village of Santa Marta turn right at sign *Anta*. Take central road of immediate fork and go ca. 1.5 km to T junction. The dolmen is on the left behind you as you face the T. The tombs are close by.

Monte Mozinho, Cidade Morta, Penafiel

Penhafidelis is located on the road going S of Duas Igrejas. The Turismo bureau will provide maps and information concerning locations in this area of petroglyphs and anthropomorphic tombs as some are difficult to find.

Sanfins de Ferreira

Citânia de Sanfins. Remains of a vast Celtic Iron Age hilltop city dating back to the sixth century B.C. with scores of circular and rectangular stone houses, remains of three defensive walls, stone rings for tethering animals, streets, drainage, cisterns, and a necropolis, the latter on the summit of the hill. The site has been extensively excavated. The central road, four metres wide in places, provided the axis upon which minor roads converged. The houses formed various nuclei of four or five units, each with its own walls and opening onto a central patio.

At the bottom of the hill a bath in the native tradition has been unearthed and about 500 m away, a Roman inscription on a rock, attributed to the third century, gives the name of the inhabitants of the town as the Fidueneae. The sequences of coinage found in the settlement continue into the fourth century A.D.

Sights:

Very large Iron Age city with remains of houses, walls, streets, cisterns, tethering rings, drainage systems, cemetery, baths, Latin rupestrian inscription. Museum below in town.

Location:

Sanfins is NE of Porto and NW of Paços de Ferreira. If coming from Santo Tirso, take the road for Guimarães and turn off for Paços de Ferreira just after the large bend in the road to the right on the edge of town. (Easy to miss.) Go ca. 13 km from turnoff to sign on left *Sanfins, 4 km*. Follow the road to the town of Sanfins, forking left at split and keep bearing left and uphill. Some of the forks have signs, most do not. At the T junction go left to church. A small sign, *Citânia*, leads to the top of the hill and parking area. Site on the right with a large concrete monument in the middle. If lost, ask for the Citânia.

Citânia de Sanfins, partial view

On the way up there is a sign for the small museum, which is a little off the "main" road. To regain the road, go up hill from the museum and turn right when that road ends.

São Vicente do Pinheiro

Termas de São Vicente do Pinheiro has the remains of Roman baths consisting of a small excavation of the Roman balneario in the gardens of the modern spa hotel. The Roman site is to the right of the hotel gate and can be seen from outside the fence. (See also, Penafiel).

Sights:

Remains of Roman baths.

Location:

E of Porto and S of Penafiel on the EN 106 ca. 9.5 km. The hotel, a large pink building, is on the right behind the taxi stand.

Vila do Conde

Remains of Celtic settlement of Cividade de Bagunte. This citânia, unmarked and hidden among the eucalyptus trees amidst the brush and foliage on the hill, has been partially excavated revealing circular and rectangular remains of structures, remnants of defensive walls and some unidentifiable remains one of which seems to have been the base for a statue. There is not a great deal to see and it is difficult to find. We were guided by three boys from the village. Close by, up the valley of the river Ave, is a Roman bridge.

Sights:

Sparse remains of a Celtic castro including remnants of walls, foundations of dwellings. Nearby Roman bridge.

Location:

Vila do Conde is N of Porto on the N 13 ca. 14 km. Take the road toward Santo Tirso E out of Vila do Conde and proceed 6 km to Vilarinho. Turn left at square and go straight (passing by castle on right) 5 km to right turn signposted Bagunte. Turn right and follow road into town ca. 500 m and church will be in front. Turn left by statue with a cross on it in centre of town and continue along this road 1.5 km to concrete wall on left with two iron gates, ca. 20 m apart. Go through first gate (on foot) and climb hill following an overgrown path approximately 300 m. To reach the Roman bridge over the river Ave, go 4 km further up the valley and the bridge is on the right.

Other sites and sights in the district of Porto include:

Lousado

Roman or Romanesque bridges are situated at Vilela near Aveleda a little southeast of Lousado on the river Sousa and another reputed Roman bridge lies further south over the same river near Meinêdo. In the church of S. Miguel of Lousado is a stone lid of a coffin with crude engravings of a human figure and two crosses that is said to date back to the seventh century. The stone tower in Lousada known as the Torre dos Mouros dates back to probably the twelfth century.

Matosinhos

Two Roman bridges situated in the surrounding countryside, along the Leça valley at Santa Cruz de Bispo, Ponte de Guifões and Ponte do Caro. Suburb of Porto.

Rebordela

Reputed rock engravings but apparently little or nothing remains. 10 km SE of Amarante in a large chestnut wood.

VIANA DO CASTELO

Afife

Mamoa de Eireira, dolmen. Partially excavated, the dolmen dates back to the third millennium B.C. It is fenced and the reputed engravings are not easily visible from a distance. The corridor is in full view but the capstone is missing.

Sight:

Dolmen.

Location:

N of Viana do Castelo on the N 13 ca. 9 km to entrance to Afife. Continue on the highway and from the first entrance into the village go 2.9 km to a large bend in the road. Here, turn left onto a dirt roadway and proceed for 100 m. Dolmen is on the right. Permission to enter the compound and see the stone engravings would be required from the Câmara Municipal in Viana do Castelo.

Castro Laboreiro

Remains of an early eleventh century castle built high on a precipice and entailing a hike up a steep pathway. Its lofty perch presents excellent views over much of the countryside including Spain.

There are also reputed megalithic tombs throughout the area but none are signposted. (Check at Câmara Municipal at Megaço.)

Sights:
Eleventh century castle.

Location:
Castro Laboreiro is in the extreme NE of Viano do Castelo near the Spanish border, reached by following the N 202 climbing S on a narrow, winding, high road from Melgaço for about 28 km. The remote mountain town is of Roman origin.

Facha

Castro de São Estevão. Very small castro on top of a hill by the church with the remains of about half-a-dozen circular houses and extensions of possible antechambers. Part of one internal wall ca. half a metre high. There is actually very little else to see.

Sights:
Castro with remains of dwellings, part of a wall.

Location:
The site lies E of Viana do Castelo. Take the road from Ponte de Lima going S toward Barcelos as far as Facha (ca. 6 km). Continue 2 km more to sign for *Castro*. Turn right and follow road 3.5 km then go left at fork and go up paved road 900 m. Small sign for castro on right. Follow narrow dirt and cobblestone path straight up hill 500 m. Stop in large open area. Castro is on the right.

Geraz do Lima

During remodelling of the Church of Santa Maria de Geraz do Lima, archaeological remains of ceramic material and of features of construction were discovered around the building relating to pre-Roman, Roman and Medieval times. Numerous graves dating from the sixth century to the end of the Middle Ages were also uncovered which seem to have constituted the cemetery of a Paleo-Christian church.

Sights:
Various ancient and Medieval structural remains around the church including tombs.

Location:

Geraz do Lima lies close to the right bank of the river Lima E of Viana do Castelo about a dozen kilometres. Turn off left (E) from the E 01/N 13 just S of Viana do Castelo onto the N 203 and proceed ca.11 km to the turnoff for Geraz.

Ponte de Lima

There are several reputed Roman bridges in this area. A portion of the long Medieval bridge in town here over the Lima river is Roman but rebuilt in the fourteenth century and restored in the fifteenth. Five arches of the original construction remain. The Roman part, today on dry land, has been extensively repaired. There are also two rebuilt Roman bridges nearby, Ponte da Geira and Ponte do Arco at Arcozelo, 2 km N of Ponte de Lima on the N 201.

Sights:

Roman bridges.

Location:

Ponte de Lima lies E of Viana do Castelo approximately 23 km on the N 202.

Roman military column, Rubiães

Rubiães

Across the Rio Coura is a pretty little Roman bridge of one main arch and smaller side arches. There is an inscribed Roman military column and other inscriptions nearby.

Sight:

Roman bridge, military column and inscriptions.

Location:

Rubiães is NE of Viana do Castelo and N of Ponte de Lima ca. 22 km. Take the N 201 S out of São Pedro da Torre toward Ponte de Lima. Go through São Benito and 3.4 km down the hill is a sign pointing W to

Roman bridge, Rubiães

Ponte Romana.. Walk down pathway ca. 150 m to bridge. For the other sights, continue on the same road 1.4 km to Romanesque church, on the left. In front of the door is the military column with a clear inscription on it. The other inscriptions are inside the church.

Soajo

See entry under Peneda-Gerês National Park.

Viana do Castelo

Citânia of Santa Luzia. Well preserved Iron Age hilltop castro containing the remains of circular stone houses, a defensive inner and outer perimeter wall and alleyways. Some of the walls of the houses stand 1.5 m high. This fortified settlement was occupied by the Romans and continued to be inhabited down to the fourteenth century. Site is fenced and officially closed to the public but access via the gate is unrestricted. A small donation for the custodian is expected.

Citânia de Santa Luzia, Viana do Castelo

Sights:

Celtic fortified village with remains of dwellings, walls and streets.

Location:

Viana do Castelo, capital of the district, is situated on the coast at the mouth of the river Lima. The castro is on the hill above town, adjacent to the Hotel Santa Luzia. About 4 km up the

Anta da Bairrosa, Vila Praia da Ancora

hill from town one passes the basilica (seen from below, as is the hotel). Continue ca. 1 km further and turn left at *Hotel* sign. The citânia is on the left approaching the entrance of the hotel.

Vila Praia da Ancora

The well preserved Dolmen da Bairrosa is classified as a national monument. It stands partially enclosed by a stone wall. There is a plaque in the wall but it is not easily visible. The dolmen has seven upright stones, a headstone and a large capstone. Artifacts date the tomb to the Late Neolithic or about the end of the third millennium B.C.

Sight:
Dolmen.

Location:
N of Viano do Castelo 16 km on N 13. Turn onto road toward Lima and go to first crossroad. Turn left (sign says *V.P. Ancora*). Continue 300 m and sign on right points to dolmen in the field on the left.

Other sites and sights in the district of Viana do Castelo include:

Cidadelhe
Remains of a castro behind village approximately one hour's walk over steep terrain. Ask in village for guide. Cidadelhe is E of Viana do Castelo and E of Ponte de Barca just over 16 km on the N 203.

Monção
Small slightly humped Roman bridge (or could be Romanesque) at Ponte de Mouro. Monção is NE of Viana and E of Valença on the northern border with Spain beside the Minho river. The bridge is adjacent (S side) to the modern bridge below the steps of the church. There are also little-explored Roman ruins in the area of Barbeita 10 km E of Monção.

Ponte de Barca
East of Viana do Castelo some 40 km the town has a nearby megalithic monument.

São Pedro da Torre
Small one-span unspectacular, restored Roman bridge over the stream in town. São Pedro is N of Viana ca. 47 km on the N 13. Turn into town and go left on Rua da Poço. Follow this to the church and 300 m further on is the bridge.

Valença
In this once Roman town with its fortifications overlooking the Minho river and Spain, stands a Roman milestone close to the church of Santo Estêvão. It was originally near the river where a Roman road passed. Valença is north of the capital on the border with Spain.

VILA REAL

Alijó
The dolmen, Anta da Fonte Coberta, has five standing stones and the capstone in place. In the vicinity there are also several castros, one considerably Romanized situated near Favaios. Others are located near Cheires, and Sanfins do Douro. The latter two sites also have Roman bridges with a third at Caldas de Carlão. There are the remains of still another castro, that of Castro da Borneira, between Alijó and Carlão.

The rupestrian paintings of Pala Pinta consist of red coloured solar symbols, a series of dots and other marks of unknown values. There are also said to be rock-cut engravings at Pegarinhos, north and east of Alijó some 18 km. These are extremely difficult to find and a guide is recommended.

Sights:

Dolmen, castros, Roman bridges, rupestrian paintings.

Location:

Alijó lies ca. 45 km to the E of Vila Real on the E 82/N 312. The dolmen is situated N of Alijó off the N 212 just W of Chã at Vila Chã.

Favaios lies a little to the SW of Alijó. Sanfins do Douro is a little NW of Alijó on a secondary road. Cheires is SW of Sanfins do Douro 3 km on secondary road and Carlão is located E of Chã (when road forks, take the right).

The paintings of Pala Pinta are difficult to find without a guide. For those who want to try it alone, however, go out of Alijó to Carlão (via Chã) 11.5 km and go left at sign for Caldas and continue through village up past the church and out into boulder-strewn vineyard country for about 2 km. After a bend in the road to the right with vineyard on left, take the dirt path to the right through trees for 2.2 km. At the T junction with vineyard in front, go left to a triple fork and take the centre way. Park on the left by the next dirt path under the tree and walk down about 300 m toward the river below. The small rock shelter with the paintings is on the right.

Boticas

The Castro de Carvalhelos, ruins of an ancient fortification or oppidum probably of Celtic origins that during the Roman occupation became a mining centre. It is situated on a rocky bluff above the river, surrounded by a wall some 2 m in diameter. On the unprotected side of the settlement there are remains of further extensions of the outer wall as much as 3 m thick. Within the compound are the foundations of a few scattered round and rectangular houses. The site is clean and well maintained and of easy access by hard-packed dirt track.

Nearby is located a Roman bridge of four spans.

Sights:

Castro with remains of walls, foundations of houses and Roman bridge.

Location:

Due N of Vila Real and W of Chaves. Leaving Chaves go 21 km on the N 103 to Boticas, then 9 km on the N 311 to Carvalhelhos. Take road into town and go through, passing factory on right. Ca. 300 m further on is a sign for the castro. Turn left and proceed uphill 1 km.

The Roman bridge is 2 km before Carvalhelhos (coming from Boticas) on the right side of road just beside and below the new bridge.

Carrazedo de Alvão

The dolmens of Carrazedo reported in some tourist literature are hardly worth a visit. The only remains are one or at most two standing stones with the remainder a pile of broken stone. Below Carrazedo on the road to Gouvães are three such derelicts and another above the town. Besides these, on the plateau of the Serra do Alvão are various clusters of dolmens, mostly in ruins, ten at Chã da Arca, five at Lixa de Alvão, four at Portelo da Chã, six near Penedos Alvos, and others at scattered sites.

Sights:
Remains of dolmens.

Location:
Carrazedo is located N of Vila Real and W of Vila Pouca de Aguiar on the N 206.

Chaves

The town, Roman Aquae Flaviae, dates back to pre-Roman times but during the Roman period it was a spa and an important staging point on the road between Braga and Astorga. Later it was occupied by the Germanic Suevi.

In town, over the river Tâmega, stands a massive Roman bridge with twelve visible arches and two Latin inscribed pillars in the centre. It was constructed in 104 during the reign of Trajan.

Above the town is a castle of the Dukes of Bragança, built on the site of a Roman fortress. It was strengthened after the Moorish conquest.

Outeiro Machado is the Bronze Age cult site of Abobeleira with rock engravings which are now greatly obscured by lichen. There is a large rock covered with mainly human figures in the guise of warriors.

The remains of several hundred metres of a Roman road may be seen just off the road to Calvão. Go ca. 5 km and it is signposted on the left. About 100 m further on from this is another blue and yellow sign *Facha Castro*, an ancient Celtic settlement, now mostly rubble.

Other Iron Age sites in the vicinity of Chaves include the Povoada de São Lourenço where little remains, Povoada da Pastoria with some excavations, but difficult to find and scant remains. There are some slight remains of wall at the Castro de Loivos, but little else.

Sights:
Roman bridge with Latin inscriptions, castle on site of Roman fortress, Bronze Age cult site, Roman road, slight remains of Castro de Loivos.

Location:
Chaves is located on a plateau N of Vila Real on the N 2 ca. 64 km some 10 km from the Spanish frontier.

The prehistoric site of Outeiro Machado lies 4 km NW of Chaves. Take the road toward Soutelo which is well signposted for the site. From under the railway bridge at the edge of town, go 4 km. A sign on right points left, but go right onto the dirt road. Go ca. 1.6 km following the road left at first fork past new houses into the trees. Turn right and immediately left where there is a sign. Continue a few metres to track on the right into parking area. The large, flat rocks in front of you have the engravings.

For Loivos go S of Chaves to Vidago then E at sign for Loivos. Go to village and on the far side is a sign pointing right to the castro. Travel up dirt road 1 km (just before road forks) and park. Walk up hill on right ca. 30 m.

The Turismo office in Chaves will provide maps for all local sites of interest.

Curalha

Castro de Curalha. A relatively small site with foundations of half-a-dozen rectangular houses, some separated by narrow walkways. Entire complex surrounded by a double wall, parts of which have been reconstructed. Site on hill overlooking the Tâmega river.

Porca de Murça

Sights:

Castro with remains of houses and double wall.

Location:

N of Vila Real and W of Chaves on the Braga N 103 road 5.5 km. In Curalha follow small white sign *castro*, left ca. 1 km up dirt and cobblestone road. When road forks, take left (central one goes into football field). Park in open area and walk up hill in front. (Do not go up path on right.)

Murça

The largest of the stone boars, the Porca de Murça, and maybe the oldest dating from the third or fourth century B.C. is located here in the gardens of the public square.

Sight:

Stone boar.

Location:

Murça is 40 km NE of Vila Real on the N 15.

Poires

Roman fortified villa at Fonte do Milho dated (by coins of Augustus and Tiberius found at the site) to the first century A.D. It appears to have continued in use into the period of the late Empire. Remains of baths and rooms.

Sights:

Scant remains of a Roman villa.

Location:

S of Vila Real on N 2 ca. 25 km. It is on the border of Vila Real and Viseu districts. Site is 12 km N of Régua between Canelas and Covalinhas.

Pópulo

Castro Vale de Cunha. There is little of interest to see here except the remains of an outer wall of massive stones behind which lies a moat and the inner wall. Both walls now only partially surround the castro. The site is open, neglected, overgrown, unfenced and with an electric power pylon in the middle.

Sight:

Slight remains of a castro.

Location:

NE of Vila Real on the N 15. The site is signposted 400 m S of Pópulo on the road between Murça and Alijó. Turn E 1 km. It lies behind a sanctuary on top of a little hill next to a small chapel and fire watchtower.

Sabrosa

Originally a Bronze Age site, the Castro da Sancha preserves a small enclosure and defensive walls several metres high and 3 m thick in some places. There are also remains of several rectangular and circular houses and what appears to have been a defensive tower with steps. The castro seems to have been occupied into the Middle Ages. Open site and somewhat overgrown.

Another, castro, that of São Domingos, near Provesende, is situated on a high hill with extensive views and is difficult to reach. Inquire in town for directions. A third castro in the area, that of Sabica, W of Sabrosa in the vicinity of São Martinho de Antas has been completely destroyed.

Around Sabrosa there are about twenty mamoas but only Madorras I, near Arcã, 9 km NW of Sabrosa, has been extensively excavated.

Rock-hewn Medieval tombs are found at Touças near Vilar de Celas, slightly NW of Arcã and 12 km from Sabrosa, consisting of five graves, some doubled, dating back to the tenth and eleventh centuries. Another nucleus of a rupestrian cemetery is located at what is known locally as Chão das Velhas dated to about the same period and near Donelo, 24 km S of Sabrosa and SW of Covas do Douro, a similar grave is found at Chão dos Mouros.

There are also reputedly several Roman roads in the area.

Sights:

Dolmen, Iron Age castros, mamoas, Medieval tombs and cemetery, Roman roads.

Location:

Sabrosa is SE of Vila Real ca. 20 km on N 322 and the Castro da Sancha is about 2 km N on the N 323. Proceeding from Vila Real to Sabrosa turn left at sign marked *castro*. Follow the road to next sign, about 800 m and turn right. Go up dirt road 450 m to end. Walk up hill ca. 200 m on eroded pathway. Provesende lies 10 km S of Sabrosa off the N 323. For the other sights it is advisable to inquire locally and information and maps can be obtained from the local tourist office.

Vila Pouca de Aguiar

Povoado do Castelo de Aguiar, a ruined early Medieval castle on the site of a Roman fort at Pontido. Roman bridges and Roman gold mines in the area. Of the latter, little more than water filled depressions remain.

Sights:

Castle, remnants of Roman gold mines, and bridges.

Location:

Vila Pouca de Aguiar is situated N of Vila Real on the N 2 ca. 28 km. For the castle, proceeding from Vila Real turn left (W) for Pontido (*Castelo*). Follow road up through country of enormous boulders and just before entering village, turn left at arrow. Walk from here up path amidst huge rocks, following yellow and white markers. Precipitous journey!

The slight remains of Roman gold mines are found at Três Minas E of Vila Pouca and at Jales to the SE.

A Roman bridge is found NW of Pedras Salgadas (which is 6.5 km N of Vila Pouca de Aguiar). The road to Romanas crosses the Avelames river, in the vicinity of a large stone quarry, over a Roman bridge with modern surface and railing. There is another reputed Roman bridge further up the same road toward Bragado 6.5 km from Pedras Salgadas.

A third Roman bridge is at Cidadelha. Entering the square in Vila Pouca de Aguiar, turn right at sign for Cidadelha and go 1.5 km to small chapel. The little one-span humpback bridge is on the right.

Vila Real

At Panóias in the vicinity of Mateus or Vale de Nogueiras is a Luso-Roman rupestrian sanctuary with remains of a temple dedicated to Serapis, Moira and other gods. It includes some nearly illegible inscriptions of the third century A.D. cut into the living rock. There are also some cisterns, water channels and steps cut from the stone. There may have been several small temples erected on the rocks as post holes suggest, dedicated to various gods as the inscriptions indicate.

Sight:

Luso-Roman rupestrian sanctuary with inscriptions.

Location:

Take the road SE of Vila Real toward Sabrosa ca. 7 km. Sign on the left indicates *Panóias 1 km*. Watch for yellow sign on right in village of Assento leading to the site.

Other sites and sights in the district of Vila Real include:

Mairos

North of Chaves on the Spanish border there are prehistoric rupestrian engravings of animals but difficult to find and a guide is recommended. One may be found at the café in village. Go N of Vila Real on N 2, 64 km to Chaves, then N on N 103-5 to Vila Verde da Raia and 10 km from there on secondary road NE. Engravings are to be found on hills of Salto and Moeda 3-4 km out of the village.

Valpaços

Roman bridge over the river Rabaçal. Valpaços is NE of Vila Real on the N 206 near the border of Bragança.

VISEU

Aldeia de Nacomba

Roman road about 1 km long, some of it in a very poor state of preservation.

Sight:

Roman road.

Location:

Aldeia de Nacomba is NE of Viseu and ca. 2.7 km SW of Moimento da Beira which is on the N 226. It is on the main road and the Roman road runs behind the *Café/Mercado Por do Sol*. Walk up behind building about 100 m.

Roman road, Almargem

Almargem

Tiny village consisting of a few houses and a restaurant on the right side of the highway going north just beyond the site of a Roman road.

Sight:

Well-preserved stretch of Roman road of about 150 m.

Location:

N of Viseu ca. 9 km on the N 2 travelling toward Lamego. Shortly after the village of Bigas, about 300 m before the bridge over the river Vouga and just before the house on the left there is a path going up into the pine forest on the right. Follow the path a few metres to the Roman road. There is a blue indicator sign on the right nearly opposite the house but this is almost impossible to see from the road due to the high bank.

Antelas

Anta Pintada de Antelas. Although declared a national monument in 1990, this dolmen is almost totally destroyed. The seven standing stones are askew, the capstone over the small burial chamber about one metre across, is missing, and the passageway is visible only in outline. No rupestrian paintings are in evidence (although reported), and the excavation is filled with sand and broken stone. The roots of trees and neglect have all but obliterated the structure.

Sight:
Remains of a dolmen.

Location:
W of Viseu and S of Oliveira de Frades on the road to Reigoso. After Pinheiros de Lafões turn left on road to Reigoso. Continue about 5 km to Sobreiro and turn right on first road after entering Sobreiro. Go 900 m to just before Antelas and take dirt path on right for about 200 m to the end. Dolmen is in front and slightly to the right ca. 50 m on the other side of a low stone wall beside a stone hut.

A castro has been reported at Ribeiradio west of Oliveira de Frades on the N 16.

Arca
The Anta de Arca, a national monument, consists of three vertical standing stones and a capstone and measures about 4.5 m high.

Sight:
Dolmen.

Location:
West of Viseu, Arca is a small village of about 480 inhabitants, situated S of Oliveira de Frades ca. 18 km.

Bodiosa
Antas de Lubagueira (Antas do Fojo). One of the dolmens is interesting for the long passageway leading into the tomb but the burial chamber itself is mostly destroyed with only two standing stones. About 150 m beyond this is another completely ruined dolmen indicated by only a depression in the ground. Note the dolmens are indicated by various names.

Sights:
Dolmens.

Location:
Take the N 16 NW from Viseu toward São Pedro do Sul passing Bodiosa to Vendas de Travanca. A sign here points left up the hill to the dolmens 2 km away. Continue to another sign on the left by a stone quarry which states *Antas do Fojo*. The first is found about 200 m off the road to the left among the pines but can also be reached by automobile over a sandy track.

Bodiosa-a-Velha

A village of a few houses on the right of the highway travelling northwest from Viseu.

Sight:

A short stretch of Roman road parallel with the highway.

Location:

On the N 16 NW from Viseu going toward São Pedro do Sul a few metres E of km stone 82 stands a blue sign which reads: *Estrada Romana.* Turn in ca. 40 m and the road is visible to the left.

Carvalhais

Remains of a Romanized hill-fort, Castro da Cárcoda, with circular and rectangular foundations of houses, passageways, remnants of wall and columns. The site, with open access, is neglected and overgrown.

Sights:

Castro with houses, passageways, walls and columns.

Location:

NW of Viseu and going NW of São Pedro do Sul on the EN 227, go right ca. 5.2 km at yellow and blue sign *Cárcoda-Ruinas Arqeológicas, 3 km.* Good road until the last 300 m and well signposted until last fork. Park car here and walk up left path (the one that goes directly to the top of the hill) ca. 250 m.

Fataunços

Roman bridge, Ponte Pedrinha, still in use, and a fairly well preserved Roman road about 700 m in length.

Lusitanian inscription of Lamas de Moledo

Sights:

Roman bridge and road.

Location:

Fataunços is NW of Viseu and reached from Vouzela on a minor road going E. Pass through village turning left after church and continue 1.6 km down to river spanned by the Roman bridge. About 50 m after bridge, beside a farm house, is a path on the right. Walk up, going left at fork to reach the Roman road.

Lamas

Lamas de Moledo, rupestrian inscription in the Lusitanian (Celtic) language written with Roman script and attributed to the second or third century A.D. The text, as given by Alarção (see Bibliography) can be translated: "The Veamnicori people offer the valley of Lamates to the god Crougea Macareaicus Petranius and a pig to Iuppiter Caielobricus."

The very large stone, resting against a wall, is now under a protective shelter.

Sight:

Lusitanian rock inscription.

Location:

N of Viseu ca. 22 km on the N 2 then right (E) to Lamas. Go through village and stone is located along a narrow lane on the opposite side of the village among houses and barns. The most convenient approach is to park in the main square and walk the several hundred metres to the spot. Ask locals for the Pedra Escrita.

Lamego

Nearby, in the valley of the river Barosa stands the seventh century Visigothic church of São Pedro de Balsemão. It was somewhat remodelled in the seventeenth century. There is a Latin inscription on the wall.

There are reputed Roman bridges nearby at Mondim da Beira and São João de Tarouca.

Sight:

Seventh century Visigothic church and Roman bridges.

Location:

Lamego is N of Viseu on the N 2 ca. 70 km. Church is located 3 km NE of town. Take the road NE out of town toward Balsemão. The Turismo office in town has a map. Follow signs and go 4 km from the Turismo. The church lies on the right just before the road descends into the village. Caution: It is much more difficult to

São Pedro de Balsamão, Lamego

find the church by taking the turnoff from the Regua road where it is signposted.

For Mondim da Beira, take the N 226 SE of Lamego 12 km and a few kilometres further south on a secondary road is São João de Tarouca.

Mangualde

Citânia da Raposeira. Excavations of foundations, hypocaust, water conduits, dwellings. Around the Igreja Matriz of Mangualde are rock-cut graves. The dolmen, Anta da Cunha Baixa, with standing chamber stones, capstone and many upright passage stones is 6 km from town and well-signposted.

Sights:

Citânia excavations including foundations, hypocaust, water conduits. Rock-cut graves. Dolmen.

Location:

Mangualde is SE of Viseu ca. 12 km on the N 16/E 80. For the excavations, go down the main street toward the bottom of the hill on which stand a church

and a hotel. Pass the island and go left on dirt road by Quinta da Raposeira passing an apple orchard on the left. Take the first left onto a narrow path and the house on the right has a sign *Excavaçoes*. Go in behind the house and there is the excavation.

The Igreja Matriz de Mangualde is below the town ca. 500 m and the Orca da Cunha Baixa dolmen is signposted out of town, 6 km.

Oliveira de Frades

The Pedras das Ferraduras is a large stone about 6.5 by 3.5 m in its natural position with numerous engraved signs which may represent animals. The Pedra dos Cantinhos is a stone 2.5 by 2.5 m showing another group of diverse (some geometrical) engraved signs. Both are in the vicinity of Benfeitas. Nearby also are remains of Roman roads and remnants of castros.

Sights:

Engraved stones, remnants of Roman roads, milestones and slight remains of castros.

Location:

Oliveira de Frades is situated W of Viseu on N 16 ca. 36 km. Stretches of Roman roads are found at Santiaguinho, Postasneiros and São João da Serra NW of Oliveira some 13 km. A milestone and bit of Roman road are found at São Vicente de Lafões 3 km SE of Oliveira and remains of castros are located at Bispeira NW of Oliveira and at Ribeiradio 15 km to the W of Oliveira. Benfeitas is S and a little W of Reigoso (see also, entry for Reigoso).

Parada de Gonta

A Latin inscription in situ incised in the living rock is situated on the side of a hill called O Castro dos Três Rios near the confluence of the three rivers, the Pavia, Asno and the Ribeiro de Vila Chã de Sá. The inscribed stone is difficult to find among innumerable other granite rocks of the same kind. It measures about 6 m long and about 2 m high. The stone is broken but the writing is still legible. It seems to be a votive inscription not unlike those at the Citânia de Sanfins and Cabeço das Fraguas.

Sight:

Latin rock inscription in situ.

Location:

SW of Viseu some 14 km on the N 2. Leave main road ca. 12 km SW of Viseu and go to Parada de Gonta. Turn left at sign *Bairro Laga da Cruz* and follow the road from this turn, 900 m. Turn left and from here go 1.1 km turning left at T junction and down to river through pine woods, (first fork take right, second fork take left). At the third fork, stop and walk down path to the left. At the bottom by the river, the rock is on a hill in front of you, across the rivers. A guide is recommended to find the inscription. Ask for Pedra Escrita.

Castro dos Três Rios, Parada de Gonta.
Courtesy of J. Untermann

Paredes de Beira

Zoomorphic granite figure of a pig or boar with a Roman inscription, at entrance to the village.

Sight:

Stone boar with Latin inscription.

Location:

NE of Viseu and SW of São João da Pesqueira. Go N of Viseu to just before Regua on the N 2 and turn E onto the N 226 toward Moimenta da Beira. From there take N 323, N to turn-off E to Riodades and Paredes de Beira.

Reigoso

A village of about four hundred people with an ancient bridge and extensive stretch of Roman road. There is an inscription in the church of Reigoso relating to the foundation by the mayor and his wife of a hostelry (*albergue*) in 1195.

Sight:

Bridge and Roman road, Medieval inscription.

Location:

W of Viseu, SW of São Pedro do Sul, and SW of Oliveira de Frades ca. 11 km. Enter Reigoso and turn back left on dirt and cobblestone path opposite stone cross on the right. Go ca. 1.6 km to village of Entráguas and small church on left with large shade tree in front of it. The Roman road runs left of the church and branches in two directions one of which runs up behind the houses of the village. The bridge is a short distance from the church down the Roman road.

São Pedro do Sul, Termas de

Termas de São Pedro, Roman baths built for medicinal purposes with hot, sulphurous water. There seems to have been two bathing pools, one large and open to the sky and surrounded by a double portico of Ionic columns and another smaller covered one. The Roman building has undergone remodelling over the centuries.

Roman baths, Termas de São Pedro do Sul

Several castros reported in the area a little west of São Pedro do Sul are situated near Baiões, Castro de Nossa Senhora da Guia, and Várzea, Castro do Banho, with vestiges of walls and dwellings. (See also, entry for Serrazes.)

Sights:

Roman baths, water conduits, columns and miscellaneous stones. Castros.

Location:

The remains of the Roman baths are in town next to a small chapel beside the river and near the Centro Termal. They are easy to find. The castros, with little to see, are located W of São Pedro do Sul on the minor road EM 607-1 (branching off right from the EM 607) out of Termas de São Pedro.

Serrazes

Pedra de Serrazes, is a very large block of granite about 2.40 m high, engraved with concentric circles and other vertical and horizontal lines during the Bronze Age. Engravings have been heightened by charcoal tracing. Unfortunately some graffiti has been added in recent times.

Sight:

Bronze Age rupestrian engraving.

Location:

For the Pedra de Serrazes, NW of Viseu, take road out of Termas de São Pedro do Sul in the direction of Viseu turning left at sign marked *Serrazes* and *Quinta das Latas* on the EM 607. Keep following signs for Quinta das Latas and at almost 5 km, you pass a cemetery on the left. 800 m further on and immediately before right turn to Penso (and the Quinta), stop. Walk up path on the right past small house of concrete blocks ca. 180 m. The stone is on the left under a weather protective cover supported by four cement columns. If in doubt, ask locals for the Pedra Escrita.

Vila Nova de Paiva

Orca de Pendilhe, dolmen with ten standing stones and a large capstone, standing in a field near the village.

On one of the stones of the Orca do Juncais near Queiriga, there is a hunting scene painted in red and consisting of deer, and men with bows and arrows, accompanied by dogs. The painting is very faint.

Bronze Age engraved stone of Serrazes

Sights:

Two dolmens.

Location:

Vila Nova de Paiva is NE of Viseu on the N 229/N 323. The Orca de Pendilhe is W of the town on the N 225 ca. 12 km and can be seen on the S side of the road W of kilometre stone 80. About 200 m E of kilometre stone 79 turn left and at triple fork take immediate left and the dolmen is on the left ca. 350 m from the road.

The Orca do Juncais is located at Queiriga SW of Vila Nova de Paiva 4 km on the N 323, then S to village. Inquire locally for exact location.

Viseu

Cava de Viriato, the remains of a Roman fortified camp, established here according to some scholars by Decimus Iunius Brutus Callaicus in 138 B.C. (the year after the death of Viriatus), wrongly associated with the last stand of Viriatus, the Lusitanian leader. Other investigators have suggested that the camp was established during Caesar's campaign here in 61 B.C. Erected on a granite base is a modern bronze statue of the warrior. Little to see but the ancient earthworks which stood about 27 m wide at the base and 6 m at the top with a height of 9 m from the bottom of the moat, once extended 2 km.

Sight:

Remains of Roman fortified camp.

Location:

In town, below the cathedral. Signposted.

Other sites and sights in the district of Viseu include:

Castro Daire

North of Viseu about 38 km. There is a unique twelfth century Roman-esque hermitage at Paiva 6 km west, the Ermida do Paiva, the only church of the Order of Saint Francis in Portugal.

Manhouce

Two bridges and vestiges of a Roman road. From São Pedro do Sul take the EN 227 NW to just beyond Santa Cruz da Trapa and turn right on the EM 612 to Manhouce.

Penalva do Castelo

Ponte das Porcas, Roman bridge and remains of road. Penalva do Castelo is E of Viseu on the N16/N329 ca. 30 km. The sites are just to the west at Insua.

São Martinho de Mouros

A Romanized hill-fort and sanctuary and a partially legible inscription to a native deity. The site lies north of Viseu and east of Lamego near the south bank of the river Douro. Turn south off the N 222 on secondary road between Barrô and Resende.

Vouzela

Remains of a Roman road between Vouzela and Vilharigues. Vouzela is W of Viseu 28 km on the N 16.

Peneda-Gerês National Park

(comprising a portion of Braga, Viana do Castelo and Vila Real)

The large national park is situated around a salient of Galicia that pro-trudes into Portugal from Spain in the eastern section of the old province of Minho.

Roman milestones, Peneda-Gerês Park

Prehistoric remains found in and around the park date back to the third millennium B.C. in the form of dolmens, for example at Paradela, Pitões and Tourém in the eastern section. A good example of a dolmen is located to the right of the Mezio entrance, past the trees leaving the park. Pre-Roman castros have been excavated at Pitões and Cidadelhe, the latter near Soajo.

In the southern section of the park there is a stretch

of Roman road along the southeast side of the Vilarinho reservoir which joins the modern highway near the Portela do Homem entrance on the Spanish border. Along it are to be seen the largest number of Roman milestones in the Iberian peninsula.

According to the Itinerarium Antonini, a kind of fourth century travel guide, the Roman military road was one of two that linked Braga to Astorga, a distance of about 215 miles. (A Roman mile was equal to 1. 481 miles.) Preserved in the area are two bridges and fifty military columns or milestones, twenty-eight of which have epigraphic remains. These monolithic, cylindrical granite stones normally commemorate the emperor who ordered the construction or repair of the road.

In the village of Soajo, where the houses are built of blocks of granite without mortar, the tenth century pelourinho (pillory column) is reputedly the oldest of its kind in Portugal.

Sights:

Dolmens, castros, Roman roads, Roman milestones, pillory column.

Location:

From the Covelães entrance (13 km W of Montalegre on the N 308) access can be gained to the eastern part of the park which houses the prehistoric sites of Pitões and Tourém and Paradela.

The western park may be entered at Mezio (18 km NE of Arcos de Valdevez on the N 101 from Braga) or a few km SE at Soajo.

At the Portela do Homem entrance (on the N 308 at the Spanish border) inside the park are seven Roman milestones of various sizes up to 2.3 m in height. Going south from the Portela toward Gerês ca. 800 m, and just after the bridge, is a good stretch of Roman road on the left. From here continue 2.7 km and turn right on a dirt road toward Campo de Gerês. After 1.2 km there are ten milestones on the left and one on the other side of the road. 1.4 km further on, to the left, just before a small bridge are six more milestones. Continuing past the Barragem do Vilarinho and 2 km from Campo de Gerês at the crossroads going toward Covide, in the centre of the road, is a statue of Christ based on a milestone. It is surrounded by columns and with a wooden roof. A few hundred metres further on is a single milestone on the right.

For more details on the archaeological sites in the park inquire at the local Turismo office.

CENTRAL PORTUGAL

DISTRICTS

The districts of central Portugal are: Castelo Branco, Coimbra, Leiria, Lisboa, Portalegre and Santarém. The coastal districts of this area of the country have been well populated since the earliest times. Prehistoric caves and grottos attest to Paleolithic and later peoples while the rivers Tejo, Lis and Mondego attracted early nomadic peoples and settlers. In the vicinity of Estoril, Cascais, Sintra, and Torres Vedras are a large number of prehistoric sites.

The Romans found this area of great interest as evidenced by their remains in the cities of Lisboa, Santarém and Coimbra, the ruins of Conimbriga and Tróia, and the many ancient roads and villas that once dotted the landscape.

To the east, prehistoric sites are scattered over broad areas but here also the Tejo river along its middle course, as well as its tributaries such as the Zêzere, played an important role in attracting early peoples.

Moslem communities also found desirable living conditions in this area and established important centres from Sintra and Lisboa to Elvas in the east.

Castelo Branco

Situated along the Spanish border, Castelo Branco occupies most of the old region of Beira Baixa and is geographically the largest central district although it is only marginally larger than Santarém. The capital dates back to pre-Roman times and was occupied by Romans and Moslems in later years. The district is separated from Portalegre in the Alto Alentejo to the south by the Tejo river. The Serra da Gardunha lies just north of the capital around Fundão and the Serra do Muradal and the Serra de Alvelos to the west. The steep southern rim of the Serra da Estrêla protrudes into the district around Covilha to the north. East and south of the capital, the landscape is less hilly, more rolling. Of the various archaeological sites in the area one of the most interesting is from Roman times at Idanha-a-Velha. Near Belmonte is the great Roman monument of Centum Cellas and there are remains of a Jewish quarter in the town.

Coimbra

The district comprises the central region of Beira Litoral with the Mondego and the Alva rivers arising in the Serra da Estrêla to the east, merging, and flowing westward to the sea at Figueira da Foz. The Serra de Buçaco lies to the north of Coimbra, the capital, while to the west the land flattens out to the

Atlantic coast. After Roman and Suevi occupation, the capital, which was situated on a hill with good views of the surrounding countryside, fell to the Arabs in the early eighth century and remained a frontier town of the Moslems until the eleventh century. Conquered by Ferdinand I of Castile and León, Coimbra was annexed to the county of Oporto. In 1187 it became the capital and remained so until the thirteenth century when the capital was transferred to Lisboa. Megaliths are well represented in the district, especially at Seixo da Beira and Fiais da Beira where there are fine dolmens. Roman remains include the cryptoporticus in Coimbra and nearby Conimbriga, one of the finest Roman archaeological sites in the country.

Leiria

This district makes up the southern portion of Beira Litoral and the capital lies on the banks of the river Lis, about twenty-two kilometres from the sea. The town was once situated on the Roman road between Olisipo and Bracara Augusta (Lisboa and Braga). While the most impressive structure in the district may be the fourteenth century Abbey of Batalha, there are important ancient sites in the vicinity such as Roman roads, bridges and the Visigothic chapel near Nazaré.

Lisboa

Encompassing much of the old Estremadura, that is, the area west of the Tejo estuary, Lisboa is the smallest of the districts but currently has the largest population. The Sintra mountains make up the highest part of the area to the west between the city and the sea. To the north the land is hilly while to the east and south across the Tejo it flattens out into extensive cork-tree forests.

The Roman settlement on the earlier site of Olisipo (Lisboa) was taken by the Suevi in A.D. 468 and remained part of their realm until the Visigoths attached it to their kingdom in the seventh century. In 717 the Arabs conquered the city and changed the name from Roman Felicitas Iulia to Al-Ushbuna, later modified to Lishbona and eventually to Lisboa. In 1147 it was conquered by a Portuguese army and fleet aided by a diverse group of crusaders. In 1256 Afonso III established his capital here. The archaeological record is well represented in this district and some of the most interesting places include the Chalcolithic sites of Leceia (Oeiras) and Zambujal (Torres Vedras), ancient burial chambers at Estoril (Alapraia), Roman villas such as Almoçageme and Odrinhas, and the Medieval rock-cut tombs at Vila Franca de Xira.

Portalegre

Filling most of the northern part of the old Alto Alentejo, Portalegre has currently the smallest population of the central districts. To the east stands the Serra de São Mamede and to the north is the hilly country around Marvão and Castelo de Vide while to the south and west the land is flat or rolling hills. The district is the northern extension of the vast undulating plain of the Alentejo, the granary of the country even in Roman times. It is watered by the river Aronches arising in the hills near Marvão and emptying into the Guadiana, by the Nisa, a tributary of the Tejo, and by the Seda and the Sor flowing westward into the river Sorraia and eventually into the Tejo. Good examples of dolmens are to be found at Aldeia da Mata, Barbacena and Nisa. Roman remains such as bridges are at Vila Formosa and the splendid villa of Torre de Palma (Monforte). There is an abundance of Visigothic and Medieval cemeteries including those at Vale do Cano (Marvão) and Castelo de Vide, the latter town also housing an old Jewish quarter.

Santarém

The district occupies most of the old area of the Ribatejo. To the west of the capital is the Serra do Aire, to the east lies the Tejo valley and to the south and north the countryside consists of rolling hills. For the Romans it was Scallabis, a major trading centre in Lusitania but it derives it present name from Santa Irene, a martyred nun from Tomar, who died in 653. The capital was under Moslem rule from the eighth to the eleventh centuries and was conquered at the end of the eleventh by Alfonso VI to become part of the country of Portugal. Captured by the Almoravides from Morocco in 1111, it became the capital of a Moslem principality and a fortified alcáçer was constructed here. In 1147 the city was reconquered by the Portugese and became a royal residence. Some of the most interesting sites in the vicinity include a dolmen attached to a church at Alcobertas, several Roman bridges in the vicinity of Mação, the Roman villa of Cardilio (Torres Novas) and the Roman earthen defensive wall at Alpiarça. The excellent Jewish quarter at Tomar is the most interesting of its kind in the country.

SITES AND SIGHTS

CASTELO BRANCO

Alpedrinha

The town still preserves a stretch of Roman road but it is not in very good condition.

Sight:

Roman road.

Location:

Alpedrinha is N of Castelo Branco ca. 34 km on the E 802. Go up the stone steps into the village (opposite the sign *Estação c.f.*) and turn right. Continue up the street to the top. The Roman road proceeding uphill is to the left of the water fountain.

Belmonte

Centum Cellas is a ponderous tower-like structure of well-dressed granite blocks, considered one of the best preserved Roman monuments in Portugal. The original function of the building is not known. It measures 15.5 m by 13.27 m and 12 m high and was divided into three storeys. It stood near the confluence of the Gaia stream and river Zêzere and on the edge of an important Roman road. The walls of the upper storey were altered in the Middle Ages when it appears to have been used as a watchtower.

The Jewish quarter of Belmonte is situated just below the thirteenth century castle. It consists of two streets with some small houses constructed of granite blocks.

Sights:

Roman tower, Judiaria.

Location:

Belmonte is N of Castelo Branco on the E 802 ca. 70 km. About 800 m N of the turnoff for the town, Centum Cellas is signposted to the right. The Jewish quarter is located in town.

Idanha-a-Velha

The village crouches on the ruins of a Roman town, possibly called Igaeditania, judging from an inscription of A.D. 4, and which gave rise to the Swabian and Visigothic name of Egitania. The name and the two hundred-

plus inscriptions from the ruins which reveal a predominance of personal Celtic names suggest, along with other finds, that the town was of pre-Roman origin. Situated on a major road from the Roman capital at Mérida to Braga and in the vicinity of gold mines, the town prospered.

The city walls still standing are 754 m long and appear to have been constructed in the fourth century A.D. and restored in the Middle Ages. The town flourished in the Visigothic

Centum Cellas, Belmonte

period from 569 when it became the seat of a bishopric and minted its own coinage. It was laid waste by Moslem invaders in the early eighth century and in the twelfth century it was handed over to the Knights Templar who constructed a tower or keep (Torre de Menagem) on the base of the Roman temple. Excavations began in 1955.

The present town, although much in ruins, is of outstanding architectural interest and well worth a visit on its own. Outside the village walls there is a Roman bridge over the river Ponsul, the remains of an earthen dam, remnants of a building identified as baths, and some remains of a kiln. Most of the sights, however, are within the town.

Sights:
Roman defensive walls and portals, bridge, sixth or seventh century Paleo-Christian restored basilica with Roman columns and capitals as well as Roman, Visigothic and Arabic arches, paintings, nearly obscured, and a large epigraphic collection. Remnants of the bishop's palace and baptistry, a Medieval watch- tower that stands on the podium of a Roman temple, small stretch of ancient road, and tombs.

Location:
NE of Castelo Branco and S of Monsanto just off the N 332, near the Spanish border.

Orjais

Reputedly, two inscriptions to Banda Brialeacus are proof that this temple existed on the hill above present-day Orjais, even though there is only the podium to see today. There was a hill-fort located above this, but, again, there is nothing to see now.

Sight:
Podium of a Roman temple.

Location:
Orjais is N of Castelo Branco on the E 802/N18 a few km N of Covilha. The chapel of Nossa Senhora das Cabeças can be seen from the highway on the hill W of town. Ask locals for road up to chapel 2.2 km away. This is a narrow, steep and very rutted dirt track. The Roman remains are 50 m above the chapel.

Other sites and sights in the district of Castelo Branco include:

Alcains
There is a Roman dam near here over the Tapadas stream. Leave Alcains on the N 18 road toward Fundão, pass bridge and go left 100 m at Tira Calças. Almost nothing to see.

Meimoa
At Cabeço de Lameirão are the foundations of buildings, shafts and capitals and

Idanha-a-Velha

bases of columns. Incorporated into the bridge over the Meimoa stream are two Latin funerary inscriptions. Meimoa is NE of Castelo Branco ca. 62 km on the N 233.

Monsanto
In the parish is a weir and a Roman bridge, Ponte da Ribeira das Razas, on the road from Monsanto to Vale de Cafede. There is also a Roman bridge, Ponte da Senhora da Azenha, over the river Ponsul. NE of Castelo Branco some 40 km.

Segura
Roman bridge over the Erges river, tributary of the Tejo. Due E of Castelo Branco on the N 240 on the Spanish border.

Vila Velha de Ródão
In the vicinity, especially around Fratel and Portas do Ródão, are many rupestrian paintings along the river Tejo but about ninety percent of them are now submerged from the dammed-up water. A few can still be seen by boat along the river and several others, that have escaped the flooding, may be seen with the services of a guide. Vila Velha de Ródão is SW of Castelo Branco 28 km on the E 802.

COIMBRA

Arganil

The nearby dolmen here displays a large burial chamber that contained several sections and a corridor, but little now remains of what was once an impressive structure as it was partially destroyed by a road. The adjacent Roman military camp, also excavated, is at present neglected and overgrown with only small sections of low earthen ramparts visible. The quantity and diversity of weapons (lances, spear heads, darts, catapults, etc.) clearly indicate a military site, probably established here to protect the mines in the area. When the camp was abandoned is uncertain. The museum in town has artifacts from both of these sites.

Sights:

Nearby dolmen at Secarius and Roman camp of Lomba do Canho.

Location:

E of Coimbra on the N 342. Take the road NE out of Arganil toward Coja. After 2 km and just before the village of Secarius turn left up unpaved road at sign *Lomba do Canho*. Bear right at the next two forks. The sites are ca. 1 km from the main road near the left bank of the Alba river.

Bobadela

The dolmen of Bobadela has a well-defined passageway with most stones standing. The burial chamber is in ruins, however, and the site is neglected and overgrown.

In Roman times Bobadela was an important city, a municipium, and seems to date back to the time of Augustus. The name of the Roman town is unknown. There are currently excavations in progress in the town and remains of an amphitheatre may be seen constructed in a hollow. A lone gate/arch, presumably to the forum, still stands a short distance away but the forum itself is no longer in evidence. There is an inscription built into the façade of the church, just behind the arch.

Roman arch, Bobadela

Sights:

Poor remnants of a dolmen. Remains of Roman amphitheatre, well-preserved Roman arch. Inscription.

Location:

NE of Coimbra on the edge of the Serra da Estrêla, ca. 80 km and 3 km W of Oliveira do Hospital. Proceeding from Oliveira, 20 m before turnoff, left, to Bobadela, stop on right side of road by bus stop. Dolmen is in the trees just behind the mimosas. Roman sites are in the village.

Coimbra

The Roman name of the city, Aeminium, may be of Celtic origin. The walls around Coimbra were probably built during the period of the Late Empire with successive renovations particularly at the end of the ninth century. Of the Roman city the forum, a triumphal arch (destroyed in 1778), and a ruined aqueduct were still present in the sixteenth century but have now disappeared. At that time the bishop's palace, built over the cryptoporticus, was remodelled and the rubble thrown into the galleries below. In the 1950s this was cleared away revealing among other things marble busts of Livia, Agrippina, Vespasian and Trajan.

Circa 580 the episcopal seat of the diocese of Conimbriga of Swabian times was moved to Aeminium under the Visigoths and Aeminium took the name of Conimbriga, becoming eventually modern Coimbra. It flourished through the Moslem period and was reconquered by Christian forces under Fernando I of León in 1047. It served as the capital of Portugal until the thirteenth century and has a twelfth century cathedral.

Roman amphitheatre, Bobadela

Sights:

Crytoporticus; remains of city walls, originally Roman.

Location:

N of Lisboa in west-central Portugal on the river Mondego. Capital of the district.

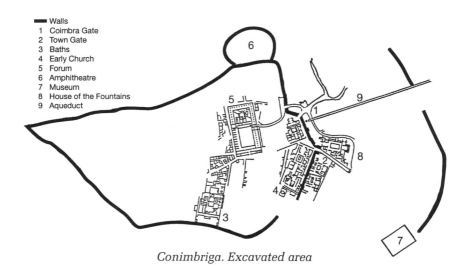

Conimbriga. Excavated area

Legend:
- ■ Walls
- 1 Coimbra Gate
- 2 Town Gate
- 3 Baths
- 4 Early Church
- 5 Forum
- 6 Amphitheatre
- 7 Museum
- 8 House of the Fountains
- 9 Aqueduct

Conimbriga

The natural defensive plateau consisting of a triangle of land between two gorges on which the site sits appears to have been occupied as early as the Neolithic period according to finds in the area. After the eighth century B.C., there are many signs of occupation and some, albeit indirect, contacts with the Tartessian civilization and with the Phoenicians. By the time of Augustus, the area was Romanized and the city of Conimbriga had acquired a new forum, baths and an aqueduct. About 3.5 kilometres away, Roman engineers discovered a source of water at a convenient height for the city, and built a dam and the aqueduct that fed the baths and fountains of the city. The construction of the forum made it necessary to demolish part of the native settlement and subsequent rebuilding of the forum finished off the remainder of the original structures. An amphitheatre was also built and is under excavation as is most of the site of Conimbriga.

During the Late Roman period the city was surrounded by walls as were other Roman cities in the west. Cisterns were also constructed in case the aqueduct suffered damage from hostile forces. In A.D. 464, according to an account by the Bishop of Chaves, the Swabians sacked Conimbriga and departed with hostages. They returned to attack in 468 and laid waste to the city and surroundings. The site was not abandoned until later, however.

This is the largest Roman settlement excavated in Portugal with impressive remains of private houses.

Sights:

Remains of the forum, amphitheatre, basilica, houses, baths (public and private), fountains, commercial sector, water conduits, lead pipes, sewerage system, aqueduct, defensive walls, gates, roads, mosaics, statues, temples, columns, cisterns, bishop's palace, ongoing excavations. Museum in situ.

Location:

Conimbriga is situated SW of Coimbra close to Condeixa on the N 1. Signposted.

Fiais da Beira

A good specimen of dolmen with most stones in place.

Sight:

Dolmen.

Location:

Take the N 17 E of Coimbra to Oliveira do Hospital. From here go ca. 15 km N to Ervedal da Beira, then W to Fiais. Dolmen is signposted.

Lourosa

The tenth century church of São Pedro (restored), unique in Portugal, was probably constructed by Mozarab artisans and contains a central nave and side aisles divided from it by broad horseshoe arches. In the entranceway are Visigothic motifs and outside are rock-hewn graves.

Conimbriga, mosaic

Sights:

Tenth century church and rock-cut graves.

Location:

NE of Coimbra on the N 17 ca. 68 km. Church is in the centre of the village.

Conimbriga, partial view.
Courtesy of Bryan Pryce

Rabaçal

Roman villa of Moroiços, currently under excavation begun in 1985 and displaying octagonal atrium with peristyle. Two large rooms are surrounded by numerous smaller rooms. The excavated area is small with much of the site yet to be uncovered. Good mosaics but they are currently under a protective covering of sand.

On the hill in the nearby town of Penela stands an imposing twelfth century castle.

Sights:
Roman villa under excavation with atrium and peristyle, foundations of rooms, mosaics.

Location:
S of Coimbra. Go to Condeixa and from there take road toward Penela (which passes Conimbriga). From Conimbriga continue 5 km and turn right just past bus stop on the left. Road not marked or signposted. Travel 5.5 km to entrance of tiny village of Ordem (Rabaçal is a larger town, just beyond). Turn right and follow narrow road up past a few houses to water tank on the right. Walk in on path on the right, forking right. Excavations ca. 100 m beyond and beside a small brick hut among the olive trees. If in doubt, ask for ruinas romanas.

Seixo da Beira
The nearby dolmen has four standing stones, remnants of a passageway, and an enormous capstone.

Sight:
Dolmen, Anta da Arcainha.

Location:
NE of Coimbra. Go on the N 1 to Santa Comba Dão, then take the N 234 to Canas de Senhorim and turn SE to Seixo on the N 231-2. Follow the road through town going toward Oliveira do Hospital. Dolmen is signposted just out of town. It is 1.2 km off the road but easy to find. There are various other remains of dolmens in the area.

Other sites and sights in the district of Coimbra include:

Antanhol
Roman camp, Mata Velha, with earthworks and trench, partially destroyed to build the airport, situated at S end of Coimbra airport. At the best preserved section, it is 28 m thick at the base and 6 m high from the ditch.

Anta da Arcainha, Seixo da Beira

Ferreira-a-Nova

A proto-historic settlement, Santa Olaia, whose artifacts show continuing habitation from the period of Phoenician and Carthaginian colonization of the Iberian peninsula into Roman times. W of Coimbra, go to Figueira da Foz and take the N 109 14 km N to Castenheiro then turn right (SE) for Ferreira-a-Nova. Little now to see.

Midões

Ponte de Sumes, a probable Roman bridge of one arch over the River Cavalos. Midões is NE of Coimbra and NW of Oliveira do Hospital on the N 384.

Montemor-o-Velho

Perched above the town is a castle rebuilt in 1088 enclosed within a double circuit of walls with imposing battlements and towers, located W of Coimbra ca. 30 km on the N 111.

Soure

Remains of the first Knights Templar castle in Portugal dating back to the early twelfth century. Soure is SW of Coimbra on the EN 342 and 14 km from Condeixa. The castle is in town.

Tábua

A well-preserved stretch of Roman road, Pedra da Sé. NE of Coimbra and a little W of Oliveira de Hospital on the N 337-4.

LEIRIA

Alcobaça

The abbey of Alcobaça (the name derives from the rivers Alcoa and Baça) has been considered by some as the best example of Medieval architecture in the country. It was founded by Afonso Henriques about 1153 to fulfill a pledge made when he conquered Santarém from the Moslems. Work on the original structure began in 1178 and was completed in 1223. Pillaged by the French in 1810 and again during anticlerical rioting in 1834, the building has undergone various restorations. There are also some slight remains of a Moorish castle in town.

Sights:

Cistercian Abbey, ruins of an Arabic castle.

Location:

Alcobaça is SW of Leiria 31 km on the N 1/N 8.

Nazaré

Nearby Visigothic church situated in the back of a farm, littered with farm implements and used as a stable. Inside may be seen several pillars with Visigothic capitals, horseshoe arches and doorways. Building is in a sad state of repair.

Sight:

Seventh century monastic church of São Gião.

Location:

Nazaré is SW of Leiria on the coast. Go 4 km S of Nazaré on the coastal road toward São Martinho do Porto. Cross bridge over the river and immediately turn right on dirt track. Continue 2.1 km to farmhouse at end. Church is directly behind farmhouse, but ask permission to see it.

Porto do Mós

A small Medieval town with a castle built on a Roman site. It was captured from the Moslems by Afonso Henriques in 1147 and re-modelled as a palace in the fifteenth century. In the vicinity near Alqueidão da Serra is a well-preserved stretch of Roman road.

Sights:

Castle, Roman road.

Location:

São Gião, Nazaré

Porto do Mós is S of Leiria ca. 20 km on the N 1/N243 and ca. 7 km S of Batalla. The castle is in town. There is also a Turismo office in town which will direct you with more detail to the Roman road which can be found by taking the road to Castelo and following signs for Alqueidão da Serra. Just before village take the left fork ca. 5 km. Ask for estrada romana.

Other sites and sights in the district of Leiria include:

Leiria

Capital of the district. The imposing castle is said to have been originally constructed by the Arabs on what may have been a Roman site. It was rebuilt in the twelfth century by Afonso Henriques and again in subsequent times. The bridge over the river Lis is reported in some travel guides as Roman but this is not confirmed by the archaeological record. Roman inscriptions in the city, embedded in some buildings, have been thought to have originated elsewhere. There is an excellent Roman statue on display in the Turismo Office. It was found in the ruins of São Sebastião do Freixo, Batalha.

LISBOA

Abóbada

Vila Romana de Freiria. Fairly extensive excavation. Centred around a peristyle, the villa lies on a gentle slope facing southeast down a valley with hills to the south and east. Some of the interior walls of the rooms are over a metre high. The granary here is the best preserved in Portugal, and there is also a wine/oil press and a grave. The remains of an altar to a native deity, Triborunnis, is now in the Museu Conde de Guimarães, Cascais.

Sights:

Roman villa with interior walls, steps, water conduits, storage bins, wheat-grinding platform and large millstone, grave, remnants of altar.

Location:

Site lies W of Lisboa. Leaving Oeiras, a little W of Lisboa on the coast, travel toward São Domingos de Rana and out on the road to Abóbada. There, follow signs for Sintra and go to the SOPLACAS pavement factory at the top of the hill.

Roman villa of Freiria, Abóbada

Continue down the hill ca. 600 m to the Café Polibar. Turn right down unpaved track opposite the café and take the right path at fork. Proceed about 300 m from the highway and site may be seen directly in front.

Almargem do Bispo

Chalcolithic Age site of Olelas. Slight remains of two round stone structures, possibly defensive towers, of a passageway and of a small bit of wall. Site neglected and little to see.

Sight:

Scant remains of Copper Age site.

Location:

NW of Lisboa. From Sintra take the road toward Mafra. Pass through village of Sabugo to top of hill and turn left at sign for Almargem do Bispo. Go 3.7 km and take lower road left at split. Immediately at next split do the same and park in front of the Junta de Freguesia. Proceed on foot up the path directly behind, past small apartment building and continue on it ca. 1 km taking left path at fork. Head for rocky summit of hill with a geodetic marker. Site is on level ground just before the marker on the right. Excellent views.

Almoçageme

Ruinas Romanas de Santo André de Almoçageme, site of a late Roman villa. Remains of various rooms, a pool and a kiln. There are several mosaics, some of the best in the country. At present the area is fenced and closed to the public but it is expected to be opened when the excavations, begun in 1985, are finished. Artifacts are currently in the Sintra museum nearby.

Sights:

Roman villa with foundations, pool, kilns and mosaics.

Location:

W of Lisboa. From Sintra take the N 247 to Colares. After passing through the town, go about 3 km toward the coast and turn right at sign for Almoçageme and *Camping.*. On the left after just a few metres is the road to Praia da Adraga. About 150 m beyond this road is the excavation on the right.

Amadora

Grutas Artificiais do Tojal de Vila Chã. Three grottos of the same architectural design, similar to those of Alapraia. (See Estoril.) The material found at the site, such as ceramics, limestone and bone idols, and metal objects, can be found in the National Museum of Archaeology and Ethnology in Lisboa.

Sights:

Three man-made grottos used as burial chambers.

Location:

Amadora is NW of Lisboa near Queluz. The grottos are reached from the road that leaves from Rua Pedro Alvares Cabral (Bairro da Mina). The grottos are located next to the EPAL depository.

Armôs

Roman fountain with inscription, situated down a flight of stairs in a small concrete structure with padlocked wooden door. The key may be obtained at the marble factory across the street. The key keeper reports that the uninspiring site, at present full of mud and debris, is scheduled for improvement.

Sight:

Roman fountain with inscription.

Location:

Armôs is NW of Lisboa and 7 km out of Sintra on the N 9 (toward Mafra). It is 3 km S of Pero Pinheiro. Turn onto road toward Armôs, and go to marble factory at the end of the village for key.

Carenque

Located here was a megalithic monument, Galeria Coberta de Carenque, hewn from the rock forming a rectangular chamber and dating back to the end of the Neolithic period. The site is now partially destroyed and there is little to see.

Sight:
Megalithic burial chamber.

Location:
The site, NW of Lisboa near Queluz, is situated beside a quarry and landfill in Bairro do Pego Longo. It is difficult to find without a guide.

Cascais
There are prehistoric grottos in town in the Jardim Visconde de Luz, but they are currently closed to the public. Little can be seen behind the iron grillwork.

There are several Roman villas in the area: O Povoado Romano dos Casais Velhas, partially excavated, displays remains of small baths, a hypocaust and the remnants of an aqueduct. The large number of murex shells and tanks found here, suggest the villa was engaged in the dyeing of purple cloth. It was occupied until at least the fifth century A. D.

The Vila Romana do Alto do Cidreira in Alcabideche contains a hypocaust, remnants of baths, water canals, tanks and mosaics, but it is difficult to find and may not be open to the public. Enquire at the Museum of Cascais.

Sights:
Grottos and remains of Roman villas.

Location:
For Casais Velhas take the N 247 road from Cascais out to Praia do Guincho and turn right at *camping* sign. Go up road toward campground but turn left some 400 m before the campground itself on Rua de São Rafael. Follow the road 300 m and Vila Vimioso is on the right. Walk up path opposite on the left. Excavations will be on your left.

The villa Alto do Cidreira is located next to the geodetic marker *João Cidreira* at the south entrance to Carrascal from Alvide. An approach to the new highway goes through the villa unfortunately rendering it hard to locate.

Catribana
Over the Bolelas stream is a single-arched Roman bridge which is in fairly good condition. Near the bridge, on the south side, is ca. 50 m of a well-preserved road which is possibly Roman.

Sights:
Roman bridge and possible Roman road.

Location:
Catribana is NW of Lisboa and N of Sintra. Take the N 247 N past Odrinhas and go left on road toward Assafora. The site is located on a hard-packed dirt road leading from the public fountain square in Catribana toward Assafora.

Cheleiros

Roman bridge, Ponte de Cheleiros. Small, single arched, humpbacked bridge probably of Roman origin, recently restored. Nearby are Paleo-Christian inscriptions on the walls of the chapel of Cheleiros.

Sights:

Probable Roman bridge and Paleo-Christian inscriptions.

Location:

N of Lisboa. Take the N 9 road from Sintra toward Mafra. Upon crossing the small river of Cheleiros on the modern bridge, the Roman bridge is beside it.

Estoril, São Pedro do

The Grutas de Alapraia are four man-made grottos hewn from the rock and used as burial chambers. They functioned as necropoli during the Late Neolithic or Early Chalcolithic period and were first excavated in 1917. They comprise four similarly constructed chambers consisting of a circular room and corridor with a manhole. The rich finds, including decorated campaniforme vases and a unique pair of limestone sandals are in the Museu Conde de Guimarães in Cascais. Each of the four grottos is marked by a plaque.

There are two other man-made caves (Grutas de São Pedro do Estoril), discovered and excavated in 1944 which were used as necropoli in Chalcolithic times. Two spiral gold rings, still on the fingers of the skeletons, were found here. These and other material are in the museum at Cascais.

One of the Grutas de Alapraia

Sights:

Man-made grottos used as burial chambers.

Location:

W of Lisboa. Take the Lisboa-Estoril coastal road and turn right (N) at São João de Estoril. Go across railway tracks and up to Alapraia, 300 m. Signposted *Grutas*. The grottos of Estoril are in the cliffs on the SE side of the small peninsula in front of the town. They are harder to find.

Leceia

Chalcolithic settlement, Povoada Fortificada de Leceia. Excavations, begun in 1983, have revealed a defensive wall and habitational structures. The former, originally of large limestone blocks and perhaps six or seven metres high, is now, like the dwellings, discernible only by its foundations. Neolithic artifacts also found there indicate even earlier occupation. The site appears to have been continuously inhabited for about one thousand years beginning ca. 3000 B.C.

There seem to have been three or four phases of Neolithic occupation and three Chalcolithic phases. The major construction of fortifications appears to have occurred between about 2400 and 2200 B.C. followed by a period of deterioration and abandonment about 2000 B.C. This is one of the three major Copper Age sites in Portugal along with Zambujal (Torres Vedras) and Monte da Tumba (Torrão). The material from the excavations is either in the National Museum of Archaeology and Ethnology, in the Museum of Geological Services or in private collections.

In situ are the remains of defensive walls and towers, slits in towers (through which to shoot arrows), round houses, one large house (perhaps belonging to a chieftain) with fireplace and flagstone floor, large paved circles for threshing wheat or crushing cereals, alleys, and a market place.

About eight hundred metres south of the settlement is a small volcanic conical mound, Monte do Castelo, where human remains were found in an artificial grotto that had been mostly destroyed by the workings of a quarry. Through radiocarbon dating they were found to be contemporary with the early phases of the settlement or about 2600 B.C.

Sights:

Remains of chalcolithic defensive walls, towers, dwellings, grain threshing floors, alleyways and market. The remnants of a windmill on the site are from the eighteenth century.

Location:

W of Lisboa and some 6 km from Oeiras to the N. From Oeiras follow signs for Leceia, continue through village and go out on the road toward Barcarena. Site is situated immediately after the last houses of the village on the right. Fenced. To view, contact the Câmara Municipal of Oeiras.

Leceia, Chalcolithic settlement, cereal-threshing platform

Lisboa

Capital of the country. The city dates back to pre-Roman times and its Roman name is recorded on various inscriptions as Felicitas Iulia Olisipo. Finds place the Roman site on the southern and western slopes of the hill on which stands the castle of São Jorge. On the castle hill was a pre-Roman oppidum which may have been founded by the Turdetani, judging by the suffix -ipo (and -ippo)—names characteristic of these people.

The consul Decimus Iunius Brutus occupied the oppidum and made it his headquarters for his campaigns of 139-137 B.C. The town was conquered by the invading Alans in A.D. 409, in 457 by the Visigoths and in 714 by the Moslems who fortified the city. Not until 1147 was Lisboa permanently held by Christian forces under Afonso Henriques after a month-long siege aided by an assorted contingent of crusaders sailing from England to the Holy Land.

The Roman theatre, carved into the hill during the reign of Nero, was discovered after the earthquake of 1755 but soon disappeared again as the city was rebuilt. It was rediscovered in 1960 when a building was demolished and this time was excavated. Presently it is closed to the public but is expected to be open when restorations are completed. It is situated at the conjunction of the Ruas de São Mamede and Saudade.

Other remains from Roman times are the so-called Roman baths of the Rua da Prata, a vast architectural complex of interconnected galleries dating back to the first century reign of Tiberius. The site has other possibilities: it may have served as a reservoir for the city or as a cryptoporticus related to the forum. Access to the site is by the Rua da Conceição. This underground complex is open to the public only on certain days of the year as it is normally flooded.

In the Casa dos Bicos, Rua dos Bacalhoeiros, an installation was discovered in 1981 for the manufacture of garum.

There is now not a great deal to see here of the Roman period since it was composed mostly of amphoras long since removed, but the Casa dos Bicos is itself a national monument, built in the sixteenth century. Some Roman remains and remnants of a Moslem wall can be seen on the lower floor of the house. About 70 m of the western section of the ancient wall that surrounded Lisboa can still be seen off the square of Santa Luzia. There are two Visigothic engraved stones in the northern and southern exterior walls of the Cathedral and three Roman inscriptions in the wall of an eighteenth century building nearby.

Sights:

Roman theatre, currently closed, some Roman and Moslem remains in the Casa dos Bicos, ancient walls, and the Termas Romanas open certain days of the year. Roman and Visigothic engraved stones.

Location:

In the city. Inquire at the Turismo office in the Town Hall (behind the Praça do Comércio and the Post Office) as to the possibility of viewing sites.

Odrinhas

Roman villa with a small museum in situ. The epigraphic remains within and outside the museum are considered the most complete and important in the country with about two hundred stones exhibiting Roman, Visigothic and Medieval inscriptions.

The chapel of São Miguel and a Medieval cemetery are situated partially over the villa obliterating much of the plan. There is a small room with a horseshoe-shaped apse still preserved which may have been an Early Christian (Visigothic) church, baptistry or mausoleum or, as some say, a temple. There are also the remains of a polychrome mosaic.

Nearby is a megalithic ensemble, Cromlech da Barreira, consisting of two dozen menhirs of various shapes and sizes. They are situated on a hillock and are visible to the right of the road that connects Sintra and Ericeira immediately after Odrinhas.

Sights:

Roman villa with foundations of structures, Medieval graves, cistern, remains of walls, horseshoe-shaped apse, mosaic. Cromlech da Barreira.

Location:

N of Lisboa and ca. 11 km from Sintra on the N 247. (About 10 km from Ericeira going toward

Roman villa and Medieval cemetery, Odrinhas

Sintra.) There is a sign on left of road (E) just after the village of Alvarinhos and just before Odrinhas. Take the narrow road curving to the right up through village. Site is 900 m on right from main road. There is also an entrance from Odrinhas, signposted for the museum, ca. 700 m. Menhirs are visible from the highway on the right on a hill and across a field from the villa.

Oeiras

Situated by the left bank of the Ribeira da Lage is a small cave, Gruta da Ponte da Lage, with an irregular, twisting corridor, occupied by Paleolithic man until the Iron Age. There is evidence of Neolithic burials in the grotto.

A mosaic with various geometric motifs discovered here in 1903 is situated on the ground floor of a private residence. It attests to the presence of a Roman household at the site but no other evidence has been uncovered. The mosaic is currently being cleaned, restored and prepared for the public.

Sights:

Prehistoric grotto, Roman mosaic.

Location:

Oeiras is just W of the city of Lisboa on the coast.

The grotto is located in the village of Ponte da Lage beside the bridge over the Lage stream.

The mosaic is situated at 38 Rua das Alcácimos. To view, go to the Câmara Municipal in Oeiras which will request the Centro do Estudos Arqueológicos to open the room.

Praia das Maças

Scant remains of a two-chambered tomb with long entrance passage but very deteriorated, neglected, and heavily overgrown. Little more than an impression in the ground and a small bit of wall about 2 m long and 60-70 cm high.

Sight:
Rock-cut tomb, Outeiro dos Mos.

Location:
NW of Lisboa. From Sintra take the road to Colares then follow signs for Praia das Maças 3 km. Drive into town 500 m from town sign and turn right on Rua António Garcia de Castro (opposite minimarket). Continue 100 m and turn right on unpaved roadway to base of small hill. Short walk to top through field and trees.

Sintra
Sites in the vicinity include the Necrópole de São Martinho consisting of two semicircular tholoi, partially destroyed, dating back to the Chalcolithic period. The site is neglected and overgrown and there is little to see except some stone foundations. There is even less to see of the Tholos do Monge, another funerary monument of the Chalcolithic era constructed with large blocks of stone and partially excavated. Of the original corridor, vestibule and burial chamber only some vestiges remain.

The megalithic monument, Anta de Monte Abraão, much deteriorated and stones askew, retains only a collapsed burial chamber. Visible from this dolmen, about 1 km to the north, is another one, Anta da Pedra dos Mouros, but this is in even worse condition with one stone barely standing. The stone does have rupestrian engravings representing a man and a woman, however. The Galeria Coberta da Estria, still another megalith retaining several vertical stones but no capstone and filled up and overgrown with little to see, is situated between the Anta da Pedra dos Mouros and Monte Abraão, about 150 m west, near a high-tension pylon. The Anta de Agualva retains seven vertical stones and part of the entrance passage but no capstone. It has been classified as a national monument.

Excavations at the Romanesque Capela de São Pedro, now mostly in ruins, have revealed the existence of a lower stratum dating back to the Neolithic period, the remains of an Iron Age settlement, an Arabic silo and a Medieval necropolis. The artifacts are in the regional museum of Sintra.

There is a well-preserved Roman bridge of one arch over the Bolelas stream and a fifty-metre stretch of Roman road on the south side of the bridge in the village of Catribana. The Barragem Romana de Belas is a dam, constructed in the third century A.D. but now much destroyed by the construction of the road linking Belas and Caneças. The lagoon formed by the dam supplied water to Lisboa via an aqueduct. It was 7 m thick and 8 m high, and about 15 m of its length still exists. The site is overgrown.

The Castelo dos Mouros, now a national monument, is perched on the crest of the mountains on two peaks of the Serra da Sintra above the town of Sintra. It was built or enlarged during the Moslem occupation in the eighth or ninth century and is surrounded by walls and several towers. The castle has undergone various repairs and restorations but there remains a Moslem horseshoe-arched gate, cistern and remnants of dwellings.

The Royal Palace, rebuilt and enlarged many times in the Vila Velha (Old Town) was once the residence of a Moslem prince and retains many elements reminiscent of the Moors in the architecture, Mudejar tiles and fountained patios. Sintra surrendered to the army of Afonso Henriques in 1140.

Sights:

Necropolis of São Martinho, Chalcolithic funerary monument, various dolmens in poor state of preservation, chapel of São Pedro, Roman bridge and road, Roman dam, Moorish castle with gate, cistern and house remains, Royal Palace exhibiting Moorish architecture.

Location:

Sintra is NW of Lisboa. The Necropolis of São Martinho may be reached through the Quinta da Maquia situated on the left of the Sintra-Ericeira road at the exit from Sintra. The Tholos do Monge is high in the Serra da Sintra, next to the geodetic marker of Monge, reached by a dirt track after passing the crossing to the Convent of the Capuchinos.

The Anta de Monte Abraão is near Queluz on top of the mountain about 200 m N of the geodetic marker. The Anta de Agualva is located at the Quinta do Carrascal on the left side of the road from Cacém to Agualva, 500 m after the crossroads of Quatro Caminhos (four roads).

The Capela de São Pedro is located in the park of the Castelo dos Mouros in Sintra.

The Roman bridge and road are reached via an unpaved track off the public square of the village of Catribana which is SW of Assafora and N of Sintra, just W of the N 247.

The Barragem Romana de Belas is out of Lisboa some 10 km and E of Sintra off the N 250 at km 16.4 between Belas and Caneças. The remains lie beside a stone hut.

Tituaria

Tholos da Tituaria, a funerary monument, composed of a burial chamber and corridor similar to other Chalcolithic burial sites.

Sight:

Copper age burial site.

Location:

Tituaria is N of Lisboa and W of Mafra between Venda do Pinheiro and Milharado. Take the road leaving the hermitage of Tituaria and terminating by some windmills (Moinhos da Casela). These are 20 m from the Tholos.

Torres Vedras

The nearby prehistoric walled settlement of Zambujal dates to around 2500 B.C. and was abandoned around 1700 B.C. It is situated on a hill and near the river Sizandro and the coast. The site was discovered in 1938 and there have been intermittent excavations. The nucleus of the site consists of a circular fortification, whose interior measures about 40 m in diameter, and the walls which are about 15 m thick. Along the wall were semicircular bastions with slits for firing arrows. A second wall, 8-10 m from the centre and about 2 m thick, also had semi circular bastions. A third defensive wall, about thirty m from the second with the same characteristics, has also been found. The fortifications had been modified and extended over the years while the settlement was in existence and several phases have been noted. Unfortunately, the site has been pilfered for its stones to build modern farmhouses. Along with the cultivation of cereals and raising of livestock, the smelting of copper was one of the most important factors in the economy of Zambujal although the mineral was apparently brought in from afar as no mines are known in the immediate area. The features of the early construction and certain artifacts seem to have some things in common with sites in the eastern Mediterranean and the possibility that cultural influences came from that quarter cannot be entirely ruled out.

There are also the remains of a hilltop Chalcolithic circular tomb, Tholos de Barro, near Torres Vedras but the site, 5 m in diameter, is all but destroyed with only the base intact consisting of stones 50-75 cm high and remnants of the entrance passageway ca. 4 m in length. The site is overgrown and offers the visitor little to see.

Chalcolithic settlement of Zambujal, Torres Vedras

Sights:
Walled Copper age settlement, Castro de Zambujal, and the nearby remains of a circular tomb of the same period.

Location:
Torres Vedras is N of Lisboa ca. 55 km. Leave the town on N 9 going W toward Santa Cruz. Go 5 km and after the village of Gibraltar go left at sign for Zambujal. Go up the road through the village to fork and go left onto dirt track. At the next fork keep to the right (signposted). Go to top of the hill and site is beside the farmhouse (about 3 km from turn off the main road).

For Tholos de Barro, leave Torres Vedras on the Lisboa road. Just outside of town is a sign on the right *Barro/Sanatorio, 2 km.* Follow this road up hill past the Sanatorio and turn right at the electricity tower taking the steep road up to the statue on top of the hill. Facing the statue, the tomb is to the left, in the bushes.

Vila Franca de Xira

There are about a dozen tombs beside the sanctuary of Senhora da Boa Morte high on the hill overlooking Vila Franca de Xira and the Tejo river. This is, perhaps, the most important sanctuary in the region, dating back to Roman times. The hilltop was repopulated in the Middle Ages, as witnessed by the remnants of walls and anthropomorphic graves cut from the rock in parallel rows. A Roman altar, funerary stones, Medieval stelae and other artifacts have been found here, some of which are in the Museum of Vila Franca de Xira.

Anthropomorphic graves of Vila Franca de Xira

Sights:

Anthropomorphic rock-hewn graves.

Location:

N of Lisboa ca. 40 km. Leaving Vila Franca on the N 1 go just past motorway entrance and follow yellow signs, left, *Senhora da Boa Morte*. (Do not follow signs for *Cava* where road splits.) Continue up to top of hill. The white dome of the sanctuary can be seen from the highway below (and from motorway). From the N 1 to the sanctuary is ca. 1 km. The graves are in the rocks directly in front of the building.

Other sites and sights in the district of Lisboa include:

Loures

Dolmen de Salemas, situated near the grotto of Salemas. It consists of a large chamber of six stones with some of the mamoa still present. Situated on a massif N of Lisboa on the Loures-Cabeço de Montachique road EN 374 N of Loures and near Salemas. A little W of Loures on the N 250 are the ruins of another dolmen, Anta das Pedras Grandes, in the Canecas suburb of Casal Novo, Rua Avelar Brotero, with passageway and chamber clearly visible but many stones in disarray including the capstone which has fallen into the interior.

Matacães

Three small rock-cut recesses in a low rock face used as burial places in megalithic times but there is now nothing to see except the shallow hollows themselves. N of Lisboa. From Torres Vedras take the N 9 road toward Alenquer. After 3 km is a sign, left, to Matacães. Pass through the village to Quintas das Lapas and stop by building with pillars. Walk down the path opposite, toward small church and take the first right turn. Go past a mound of large trees and caves are on the left side of the next mound.

Montelavar

A Roman road (much of which is still intact) from Montelavar, about 9 km NE of Sintra on the N 9, to Odrinhas.

Pragança

Castro de Pragança, an Iron Age site. N of Lisboa and 8 km SE of Cadaval, the castro is on the hill above the village. Somewhat elusive, but ask for it by name in the village. The hilltop was inhabited from Paleolithic times but there is little now left to see.

PORTALEGRE

Aldeia da Mata

Dolmen, Anta do Tapadão with capstone intact dates back to about 3000 B.C. Most stones are standing, but the passageway is partly destroyed.

Sight:

Dolmen.

Location:

Go W of Portalegre 21 km to Crato then W to Aldeia da Mata. At fork where one road goes to Monte da Pedra, keep on the Aldeia road and go 3.5 km. Dolmen can now be seen on left. Permission to enter the farm by car can be obtained at the farm house ca. 800 m further on, or one may walk in from the highway.

Alter do Chão

The Roman name of the town was Abelterium and one of the military roads linking Lisboa and Mérida went through it. The town was destroyed in Roman times for rebellion and was not rebuilt until the thirteenth century. The castle was constructed in the fifteenth century.

In town are the remains of partially excavated Roman baths, some remnants of structures and water conduits but not a great deal to see. Outside of town stands a dolmen.

Dolmen, Barbacena

Sights:

Remains of Roman baths. Dolmen.

Location:

Alter do Chão is located SW of Portalegre some 34 km on the N 119/N 245. The dolmen is situated on the N 245 going S from Crato about 6 km before Alter do Chão on the W side of the road. The Roman baths are in the football field in town (near the tennis courts and swimming pool).

Barbacena

Anta do Reguengo with four standing stones and capstone in place. Part of the passageway is still prominent with one overhead stone. A good example.

Sight:

Dolmen.

Location:

Barbacena is SE of Portalegre and reached by going S 29 km on the N 18 to Monforte and then SE 17 km. Beside the sign denoting the village, turn right on dirt road and proceed 3 km to quarry with what is locally known as the Ponte Romana on the right. Just past the bridge the dolmen can be seen on the right among the cork trees.

Campo Maior

Castro de Segovia with foundations of several structures and a small remnant of stone wall. The settlement is on top of a long, narrow hill and potentially important but so far there are only slight excavations. At present an unrewarding site.

Sights:

Slight remains of Iron Age settlement showing foundations and part of wall.

Location:

Campo Maior is SE of Portalegre ca. 50 km. Go out of town on the N 373 toward Elvas for 5 km and after crossing the river Caia turn left and go up unpaved road 600 m to the top of the hill.

Castelo de Vide

There are many ancient sites in the vicinity of Castelo de Vide with some twenty-eight megaliths and two menhirs (one broken) in the parish, although many of these have been totally destroyed or are in a very poor state of preservation. The Dolmens dos Coureleiros, for example, comprise a group of four: one consists of massive stones, some displaced by the roots of trees and others missing. It has been reinforced. Another retains part of the corridor and six standing stones but all askew. It, too, has been somewhat reinforced. Of the remaining two, one is in very poor condition and the other is almost completely obliterated with only an impression in the ground and one stone remaining. They are in the area of a quarry where dynamiting tends to shift and break the stones.

Anta do Alcogulo consists of three dolmens. One preserves five standing stones, the cover and part of the corridor. The second has no covering stone but has seven stones intact, and the third is totally destroyed with no stones in place.

The Anta da Melriça is one of the more important in the area due to its well-preserved condition with only four stones destroyed or partially fragmented. The capstone is in place but there is no evidence of the corridor.

Anta do Sobral is a fairly small but good example of a dolmen composed of seven stones and cover, and an irregular polygonal chamber. It does not seem to have had a corridor.

Anta dos Mosteiros is the largest dolmen in the vicinity but is not in good condition. There is a passageway and six enormous standing stones (one broken off), and the headstone and some of the chamber stones are lying on the ground.

The region around Castelo de Vide is also well-endowed with Roman and Visigothic remains, anthropomorphic sepulchres and *chafurdãos* (stone, circular buildings with roofs of straw whose origins are uncertain but which are reminiscent of those at the Citânia de Briteiros). There are some 100 or so of these in the vicinity, said to be Medieval but probably much older.

At the site of the Roman Villa dos Mosteiros, while there is little to see of the unexcavated villa apart from some fragments of walls, and the walls of a monastery constructed with Roman stones from the villa, there is a rare specimen of a Roman kiln.

The Necrópole de Santo Amarinho is a Visigothic cemetery of stone-made sarcophagi. Two medieval rock-cut graves are nearby along with a *chafurdão*. The area around these sites was once a Bronze Age habitat but there are now only a few miscellaneous stones left to see from that period.

Judiaria, Castelo de Vide

Another Medieval cemetery in the vicinity is that of the Necrópole da Azinhaga da Boa Morte at the Barragem of Póvoa e Meadas which contains about nine graves. Site is fenced but easily visible.

The town of Castelo de Vide was occupied by the Romans in about 44 B.C., destroyed by the Vandals in 411 and in 713 seized by the Moslems. The town was reconquered by Afonso Henriques in 1148. It preserves the Medieval Jewish quarter and synagogue, formerly a house and currently in poor condition. Of interest also is the typical private house, Casa do Arçário, somewhat restored, the Casa da Rua Nova, a private house, constructed at the end of the fifteenth century, the Casa do Rabi or Rabbi's house built in the sixteenth century and the sixteenth century Forno Judaico (Jewish oven), used until recently to bake bread and cakes. The Fonte da Vila (fountain) of the fifteenth century, the focal point of the quarter, is still in use.

The Jewish quarter was well-established in Castelo de Vide by 1455 and expanded by exiles from Spain in 1492 when they were expelled from that country. In 1497 they underwent forced conversion to Christianity or deportation. The Casa da Rua Nova appears to have belonged to the first Jewish convert in town.

From the Moorish period of the massive castle overlooking the town there remains only a system of ventilation.

Sights:
Dolmens, Roman kiln and traces of villa, Visigothic and Medieval cemeteries, *Chafurdãos,* Judiaria.

Remains of a Roman kiln near Castelo de Vide

Location:
Castelo de Vide is N of Portalegre approximately 20 km. For the dolmen of Melriça take the N 246 out of Castelo de Vide toward Alpalhão, pass the turnoff, left, for Portalegre and continue 1.9 km (to between km stones 11 and 12). Dolmen is on the right, close to a house and visible from the highway where it is marked by a blue sign. It is just before the small secondary road off to the right that leads to the Barragem da Póvoa.

For the Dolmen do Alcogulo take road from Portalegre toward Alpalhão. Go 14 km, and turn right (E) at Alagoa. Pass through village and take the road marked Castelo de Vide, the left fork. (This shorter road at present cannot be taken from Castelo de Vide as it is sealed off at that end.) From fork, travel 5.3 km to where the RR line crosses overhead. Between 700-800 m beyond the RR bridge enter the field on the left through gate in barbed wire fence and walk along the property-dividing stone wall on the right. (Going W.) The dolmen is ca. 500 m among some trees and against the other side (N) of the wall. About 200 m NW of this dolmen is another in poor condition and 500 m beyond that is a third, totally destroyed.

On the highway N 246 out of Castelo de Vide going toward Alpalhão, and a little way out of town, turn right at sign for Póvoa e Meadas on secondary road. Go 1.5 km and turn right. Go a further 1 km crossing RR track and turn left on dirt track. Continue 400 m to first dolmen of Coureleiros beside the road on the right. About 50 m further on is a second dolmen on right by a fence and near it a third, destroyed. About 300 m further along is the fourth dolmen beside a small house on the left. There is not much left of this one.

From Castelo de Vide on the road to Alpalhão turn left toward Portalegre for the Dolmen do Sobral. Just after km 16 and just past the turning to the Necrópole de Santo Amarinho the dolmen can be seen on the right of the highway.

To reach the Necrópole de Santo Amarinho turn right and immediately right again after km stone 15 on the Portalegre road (N 246) from Castelo de Vide. Continue 500 m and a *chafurdão* can be seen on the left across a field. Proceed through the gate on the right (be sure to close it) and go to the next gate, cross small stream. (The *chafurdão* is now on your right.) The Visigothic Necropolis is situated in a small fenced patch of land behind the farmhouse. Ask owner for permission to view it. Two rock-cut graves are in a stone outcropping beside the house.

For the Necropolis of Azinhaga da Boa Morte leave Castelo de Vide on the Alpalhão highway and turn right to Barragem just after the dolmen of Melriça on secondary road. At 3.7 km is a *chafurdão* on the left and 1.1 km further on, 200 m from the road, between two trees and overgrown, is a dolmen but with only two standing stones and no capstone. Another 2.1 km on the left stands a small house some 200 m from the road, 20 m from which is another dolmen. About 400 m further are three anthropomorphic graves in a large stone on top of a mound on the right. Continue on, crossing over the dam. You will have come 9.8 km from the main Alpalhão highway when a dirt pathway is seen to the right. Continue on this and take first fork to the right and second fork to the left. After about 100 m stop at top of knoll. The fenced necropolis is to the right, on the margin of the dam and marked with a sign.

The Roman villa may be reached by returning along the dirt pathway to the main road from the Necrópole da Azinhaga and turning right for 1.7 km

Chafurdão

then left on the road toward Nisa. Continue 1.1 km and go right at sign for Póvoa e Meadas. After 2 km turn left onto dirt track and follow this 1.5 km (at fork continue straight, beside wall) to end of road. This is about 17 km from the original turnoff the Alpalhão highway. Walk through the gate past the hut on right and through the next gate. Veer left through the olive trees toward a white building. The excavation of the rare Roman furnace is on the left. Leaving this site, retrace steps through the last gate and into next field where there is a bit of Roman wall and the remains of a monastery. Then, follow the stone property dividing wall around to a small hillock where there are the remains of the Anta dos Mosteiros.

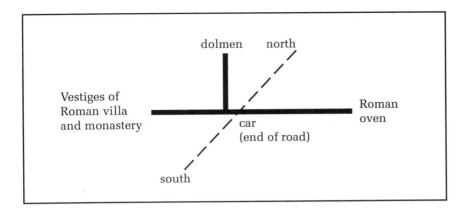

The Judiaria is in town.

Crato

Dolmen, Monte dos Andreiros, in fairly good state of preservation, most chamber stones upright, but no passageway. Roman bridges.

Sights:

Dolmen and two Roman bridges.

Location:

Crato is 21 km due west of Portalegre. For the Roman bridges, leave Crato on the N 245, S toward Alter do Chão. Crossing a modern bridge 1.5 km from town, the Roman bridge is seen to the right. Crossing a second modern bridge ca. 1 km further on, another Roman bridge is also to the right.

For the dolmen Monte dos Andreiros, continue on the N 245 ca. 3 km to the Estação. There is a signpost for Alter do Chão but instead go left in front of the station to where the road becomes a dirt track and crosses the railroad track again. Continue along this track. From the turnoff at the station to the dolmen is 1 km. Dolmen is on the left, up against a lone cork tree.

Crato e Mártires

Remains of a large Roman villa with foundations of some structures, but now little left to see.

Sight:

Scant remains of Roman villa.

Location:

From Crato, 21 km W of Portalegre go S on the N 245. Pass Estação of Crato and a short while after, a path leads left where the slight Roman remains can be seen from the road. Ask for Granja Romana.

Marvão

Scenic hilltop town with numerous and diverse archaeological sites in the vicinity. Some, hidden from view by the thickets of the hills, are very difficult to find without a guide. Several grottos inhabited from Paleolithic down to Roman times are in the area and consist of huge overlapping stones under which the earliest peoples found shelter. There is nothing left to see but the grottos themselves, however, which are located near two dolmens, and a Bronze Age settlement. (Paleolithic artifacts in the museum of Marvão.) The dolmens are about 75 metres apart and are both heavily overgrown and difficult to find. One is nearly completely destroyed, the other is in fairly good condition with capstone and passageway intact. The Anta da Bola de Cera is beside the road but mostly hidden from view by the embankment. In the hills behind it are other Paleolithic caves. The Menhir da Agua de Cuba is only about 1 metre high and stands just off the road. The Anta dos Pombais lies right beside the road.

The Povoada de São Gens, a hill-top Bronze Age settlement entails a strenuous climb through thick brush to the summit of the hill. Visible are parts of the outer wall made of large uncut stones, some remnants of inner walls, many collapsed stone dwellings, sherds and fragments of millstones.

Near the unexcavated Roman villa, Povoada dos Vidais and its reputed cemetery (nothing to see) are two Roman wine presses cut from the rock, one of which runs off into a rock-cut basin.

At Vale do Cano are Medieval rock-cut graves, some anthropomorphic, nine in a cluster and one about twenty metres away. Here also is a rock-cut wine press with two concentric circles running off into a basin.

Sights:

Prehistoric grottos, dolmens, menhir, Bronze Age settlements, Roman wine presses, Medieval graves and wine presses.

Location:

Marvão is NE of Portalegre ca. 17 km. Coming from Castelo de Vide N of Portalegre, follow the N 246-1 E turning left for Marvão and then take the left fork signposted for Beira. A few hundred metres past km stone 113 is a green sign on right pointing to the small Menhir da Agua de Cuba in field on left. It can be seen from the road.

Continue on through the village of Santo António das Areias 4.4 km to signpost for Beira. Turn left toward Beira and go 1.2 km and turn right on unpaved road. Travel another 1.2 km and park. Climb over the stone wall on the left and walk across small field to rocks. Here, on top, are the Roman wine presses.

Having returned to the car, walk up the road ca. 300 m and cut into left on the side of the first knoll. Climb up ca. 20 m to grottos. From here continue to the top of the hill behind (the same hill as seen up behind the wine presses) to a Bronze Age settlement at the summit. There is very little left to see of the ancient village, just a few scattered stones. From the summit, walk parallel to the road below keeping it on the left, for 300-400 m. In the tangle of trees and brush are the remains of two dolmens, one in a very poor state of preservation.

Descending to the car again there is to the north and in the opposite direction of the wine presses the unexcavated Roman villa and cemetery of Povoada dos Vidais. There is virtually nothing to see there. Return to the main road and go right for 700 m to a small parking area on the left. The Dolmen da Bola de Cera is directly above the embankment of the road. From here one may proceed further into the heavy growth of the hills behind and look for more prehistoric caves said to be there.

Further down the road 900 m stands the Anta dos Pombais on the right, easily seen from the car. Continue from here along the road following signs for Beira, go through the village and turn left toward Fadagosa. Go left at split. Ca. 5.9 km from the Anta dos Pombais, turn in left onto gravel roadway and take left fork. After 1.3 km, stop. (From RR crossing at Beira to turnoff is 4.9 km.) In front is a mountain, walk to the summit (about 25 minute hike through wheat field and cork trees), veer to the left, climb over the stone fence at base of hill and continue up rough, steep uncharted ground to Povoada de São Gens).

Back on the main road again, proceed for 1 km to where there is a farm on the left and sign for the concelho of Marvão facing the other way (on left). Walk up the bank on the left (there is a large rock sticking up on the right as one faces the bank) for ca. 70 m to rock-cut Medieval tombs of Vale do Cano. Then walking toward the farm to just beyond the cattle shelter of concrete pillars supporting a tin roof, you will find the wine press hewn from a rock.

Roman wine press near Marvão

Monforte

Roman villa, Quinta da Torre de Palma. The remains of the buildings of the villa occupy an area of 280 by 200 m and have been extensively excavated. It appears to have been occupied from the first century A.D. to the Visigothic period. The mosaics date back to the end of the third or to the fourth century. Ca. 100 m from the villa complex are the remains of a basilica dating back to the fourth century A.D. but altered in the fifth and seventh centuries with the addition of a baptistry. The baptismal font in a style similar to the cross of Lorraine is unique in the peninsula.

The villa shows the remains of wells, a press, a colonnaded patio, servants' quarters, grain storage sheds, various rooms around a rectangular atrium, owner's residence with buildings organized around a porticoed gallery or peristyle with a central tank (impluvium) and with adjacent rooms with mosaics as, for example, the dining room, reception room and living room.

There are also the remains of a garden area and cistern, large room for baths with hot, tepid and cold water, apodyterium, hypocaust, basilica with two apses, two Paleo-Christian cemeteries and a large building where an altar dedicated to Mars was found. In the necropolis are individual and family tombs.

There is a reputed Roman bridge close by (but could be Romanesque).

Roman villa, Quinta da Torre de Palma, baptismal font

Sights:

Large Roman villa with mosaics, wells, press, patio, foundations of rooms, gallery, cistern, baths. Paleo-Christian cemeteries, baptistry, and basilica. Possible Roman bridge.

Location:

Monforte is S of Portalegre on the N 18. Leave town on the road toward Alter do Chão. Signpost upon leaving town states: *Ruinas 6 km.* Another 4.4 km and a sign points left. Follow dirt track to fenced area with small hut at entrance. The Roman bridge is on an old road out of Monforte toward Alter do Chão and can be seen on the right just past three churches.

Nisa

In the vicinity of Nisa are the Anta de São Gens with five standing stones and capstone, an anthropomorphic rock-cut grave situated on top of an outcropping of rock ca. 2 m high, and a Roman bridge and stretch of road at Vinagra.

Sights:

Dolmen, anthropomorphic tomb, Roman bridge and road.

Location:

NW of Portalegre 35 km. Take the N 364 SW of Nisa toward Tolosa. Go 7.1 km and turn left at crossroad. After 4 km the dolmen is on the left side of the road and the grave is on the opposite side about 50 m back from the road. (From Alpalhão, dolmen is 6.1 km on secondary road.) Vinagra with the Roman bridge and road is a little to the northeast of Nisa going on the secondary road toward Pé da Serra.

São Vicente e Ventosa

Some slight excavations revealing what appears to have been a Roman villa and the floor of a small basilica with an apse. There is little to see at present except a few foundations of structures.

Sight:
Scant remains of Roman villa, Quinta das Longas.

Location:
SE of Portalegre and 8 km NW of Elvas on the N 246. Going from the village of São Vicente toward Elvas, travel 2 km and on the left is a blue sign *Quinta das Longas.* Drive up farm road 700 m to gate. Permission must be asked from the owner to see the excavation being conducted by the University of Lisboa. Facing the farmhouse, the site is on the left about 100 m near the stone wall.

Vila Formosa
Imposing six-arched Roman bridge ca. 116 m long and 6.7 m wide. Small high arches allow flood water to pass underneath. The bridge was on the road from Olisipo (Lisboa) to Augusta Emerita (Mérida, in Spain) and still carries modern traffic. It is one of the best preserved in Portugal.

Sight:
Roman bridge of Vila Formosa.

Location:
Seda is SW of Portalegre and W of Alter do Chão. The bridge is over the river Seda on the road N369/N 119 from Alter do Chão going W toward Ponte de Sor. It is located 3 km after the road to Seda turns off left.

Other sites and sights in the district of Portalegre include:

Roman bridge of Vila Formosa

Benavila
Parallel to the modern bridge is a small three-arched bridge, reputed to be of Roman origin. SW of Portalegre and just beyond Benavila going N on the N 370 toward Seda.

Elvas
Arabic castle built on Roman foundations. SE of Portalegre ca. 57 km, near the Spanish border on the N 4/E 90. The aqueduct just outside of town was begun in 1498 and rebuilt in the nineteenth century. Of the 843 arches only 371 are original.

Esperança
Rupestrian rock-shelter paintings. SE of Portalegre and NE of Arronches near the Spanish border. The grottos are in the Serra de Louções, close to the

nearby village of Hortas de Baixo and a guide is suggested as is the case for the rock paintings of the Serra dos Cavaleiros, W of Hortas de Cima.

Monte da Pedra

Remains of a Roman bridge. NW of Portalegre and W of Alpalhão on the road between Monte da Pedra and Gáfete.

São Bras e São Lourenço

Torre das Arcas cemetery with about 79 burials of the second and third centuries. Some vestiges of buildings, channels and dams. SE of Portalegre and a few km W of Elvas on the road toward Estremoz N4/E90. Ca. 1 km off the main road, but difficult to find among the trees and bushes. Locals know the site.

São Salvador de Aramenha

Little left to see here except a few metres of a Roman wall (in spite of some guidebooks' recommendations) everything removed or under ploughed fields. On road from Portalegre toward Marvão, cross bridge just before town of Armenha. A few hundred metres beyond the bridge before the road bends is a bit of Roman wall on the left.

SANTARÉM

Alcobertas

The church of Santa Madalén is somewhat unique in that a dolmen containing an altar is attached to it. The capstone of the dolmen is missing but a cupola has been built over it.

Combined dolmen and church at Alcobertas

Sight:
Dolmen forming part of a church.

Location:
To reach Alcobertas go NW of Santarém 25 km on the N 362 to Alcanede. A few km NW of here, go left (W) to Alcobertas on a secondary road. The dolmen/church is in town.

Alpiarça
Paleolithic,Chalcolithic, Bronze Age and Roman site, Alto do Castelo, above the left bank of the Tejo river. There is little to see here now except the earthenwork defensive wall which extends around a vineyard for a considerable distance, broken in places to accommodate farm roads. Artifacts from all periods are currently in the Câmara Municipal pending a museum on the site.

There were also various prehistoric cemeteries discovered in the area and Roman milestones dedicated to Trajan indicating the presence of the military road from Lisboa to Mérida. Reputed Roman dam in the area.

Sight:
Prehistoric and Roman site displaying earthen wall.

Location:
E of Santarém 10 km on the N 368. In Alpiarça follow *Camping* signs and 300 m beyond entry to campsite there is a gate on the left. Enter and continue up farm road through vineyard ca. 300 m to earthworks.

Tomar
Ancient Sellium, an important town on the road from Olisipo (Lisboa) to Braga. Small excavations of Roman ruins begun in 1981 seem to indicate that the Roman city was on the left bank of the river Nabão while the Medieval city developed primarily on the right bank nearer the castle. The town seems to have been founded in the first half of the first century A.D. Under the forum, excavated from 1981 to 1985 (but partially destroyed by the construction of modern blocks of apartments), were found remnants of an Iron Age site. The Roman cemetery for the town has not been found. The tombstones were probably re-used in later construction.

There were several rustic Roman villas in the vicinity of Tomar and one that has been partially excavated is that of Caldelas. It functioned as an agricultural establishment from the first to the fourth or early fifth century A.D. when it was abandoned or destroyed.

The Judiaria and synagogue, the latter at 73 Rua Joaquim Jacinto, were in use in the fifteenth century and next door (discovered in 1985) are the women's ritual baths under the floor of the house and now undergoing excavation. At number 40 is one of the few original houses left, now being restored, that of the guard of the Jewish quarter. The synagogue, dating back to the fourteenth century, is considered to be one of the oldest and best preserved in the country and is noted for its size and sparse decoration. It was a rectangular building with separate entrances for men and women and now houses Hebrew tombstones and inscriptions collected from various parts of the country.

The Templar's castle overlooking the city originally dates to the twelfth century but only the defensive walls and parts of the keep are from that period.

Sights:
Remains of the Roman town under excavation revealing foundations of buildings and walls and part of basilica with three naves, some remains of the forum. Roman villa with remains of dwellings and polychrome mosaics. Jewish quarter with synagogue and excavations.

Location:
Tomar is NE of Santarém 64 km. Take the N 3 to Entroncamento, 46 km and then go N for 18 km on the N 110. Most sights are in town. Roman ruins are behind the fire station off the Rua de Carlos Campeão. The Roman villa at Caldelas, 5 km SW of Tomar lies 500 m from the left bank of the river Beselga.

Torres Novas

The Roman villa of Cardílio was partially excavated in the 1960s and reopened for further work in 1980. One of the rooms off the peristyle had the inscription *Viventes Cardilium et Avitam Felix Turre* which seems to read "May Cardilius and Avita (probably the owners) be happy in their Turris (villa)." Recent work indicates that important alterations to the villa took place between the first and fourth centuries and a bath complex has been revealed in the southeastern part of the residence. Mosaics, some in vivid colour and geometrical designs, cover the floors of various rooms and seem to date back to the second and third centuries A.D.

Unfortunately, the villa has long been known and its stones carted away for the construction of local houses.

There are also the remains of a Roman road between the town and the villa.

Underground in the suburb of Lapas is a unique labyrinth of tunnels in the soft tufa rock. Their purpose and period of construction is unknown. An Early Christian sanctuary from the abuses of the Romans or Moslems? Burial chambers? Nothing remains to decide the issue. The narrow, twisting grottos seem to run off in numerous directions and are entered from a door on the street. In some places the foundations of the houses above can be seen by looking up vertical shafts in the ceiling. It would not be difficult to get lost in the maze.

Sights:

Roman villa with remains of central peristyle and surrounding structures, remnants of columns, mosaics, well, cisterns, garden area. Roman road of ca. 800 m nearby. Underground labyrinth of Lapas.

Location:

Torres Novas is NE of Santarém ca. 40 km on the N 3. For the Roman villa, go out of town toward Castelo Branco, but at fork follow sign to A 1 motorway. The villa is immediately signposted. Cross bridge and take unpaved road on left 1.7 km. The Roman road is between the villa and the town. For Lapas, about 2 km away, ask at museum in town for key and permission to visit.

Vila Nova de São Pedro

The remains of a Chalcolithic fortified village near the Tejo. Antedating the defenses was a settlement relating to the Palmela culture beginning about 3000 B.C. Over this was constructed a citadel only about 75 m across surrounded by a stone wall cemented with mud, about 8 m thick, with bastions and round towers. A second and third wall, also with bastions, ran further out. The defenses and material content link this site with Los Millares in Spain and to a date of about 2500 B.C., comparable chronologically to that of Zambujal near Torres Vedras. The site is neglected and heavily overgrown.

Sights:

Copper Age settlement with vestiges of central enclosure, walls, dwellings and cisterns.

Location:

The village is SW of Santarém and 7 km NW of Cartaxo. Pass through to the next village with a water tower, following signs *Castro*. Proceed to the hill with the remains of a windmill on it and turn right, down an unpaved roadway, past the windmill ca. 500 m. Castro is on the right.

Other sites and sights in the district of Santarém include:

Cardigos

Roman bridge, Ponte de Isna, NE of Santarém, NE of Abrantes on the N 3, and N of Mação some 23 km near the Portalegre border.

Envendos

Nearby Roman bridge. NE of Santarém, 37 km NE of Abrantes and E ca. 13 km from Mação.

Mação

Ponte da Ribeira das Eiras (or de Palhafome), Roman bridge. There is a second Roman bridge here but the date is in doubt. Mação is NE of Santarém and NE of Abrantes 27 km on the N 3.

Mosaic from Roman villa Cardilio, Torres Novas

Muge

Nearby Mesolithic shellmidden sites of which few of the originals, Cabeço da Amoreira and Cabeço da Arruda, are preserved. The large size of the middens indicate repeated or prolonged settlements in a favorable environment where both marine and terrestrial food sources could be exploited.

Some of the limestone caves in the area were occupied during Paleolithic and Mesolithic times. Muge lies about 20 km south of Santarém on the N 114/ 118.

Penhascoso

Roman bridge nearby, Ponte do Coadouro, NE of Santarém on the N 3 and just before Mação.

Rio de Moinhos

Roman excavation, Quinta da Pedreira, with vestiges of what could be a hypocaust, late Roman and Medieval burials in the ruins and foundations of structures. NE of Santarém and a few km NW of Abrantes on the N 3.

Valada

Roman road and other unspecified remains. From Santarém go SW 13 km on the N 3 to Cartaxo, continue 5 more km and turn left on the N 3-2 for 8 km. Velada is on the river Tejo.

SOUTHERN PORTUGAL

DISTRICTS

Four regions make up the southern section of the country: Beja, Évora, Faro and Setúbal. Beja is the largest geographically, encompassing the old Baixo Alentejo, and Évora, incorporating the southern portion of the old Alto Alentejo, is second. Faro is the southernmost region coextensive with the old province of the Algarve. Setúbal consists of the southern part of the provinces of Estremadura and northwestern Baixo Alentejo. It also has the highest population density, with Faro second.

The Algarve is separated from the others by a range of hills broken by volcanic rock overlying the schists and is divided from its eastern section by the rivers Odelouca and Arade which merge, along with other sometime streams from the Algarvian mountains, and flow south to Portimão on the coast.

North of the mountains are the plains of the Alentejo. Between the two regions the contrast in climate and vegetation is notable. The river Guadiana waters the eastern Alentejo and flows southward along the Spanish border for part of its journey. Flowing from southeast to northwest, the Sado river, and its many tributaries, waters the central and western Alentejo and enters the sea at Setúbal. Further south, the river Mira, like the Sado, runs along a northwest course but flows into the Atlantic Ocean at Vila Nova de Milfontes.

These southern districts were the domains of the Conii, Turdetani and the Celtici, about whom we know little. Similarly, knowledge of their commercial and social relations with the Phoenician and Greek sailors who came to trade, is at best nubilous but recent finds in Alcácer do Sal and in the Algarve are beginning to fill in the picture.

Except for the coastal areas and some river valleys, especially the Guadiana, the region seems to have been sparsely occupied in prehistoric times. Lack of good defensive terrain and predictable water in the Alentejo may help account for early man's antipathy to this area, although some mining, a major attraction, was carried out as early as the Bronze Age. With the Romans, however, keepers of the peace and master builders of aqueducts and dams, the fertile land was set to good agricultural purposes. The mines were an added inducement which the Romans knew well how to exploit.

Beja

Clinging to a low hill surrounded by the fertile plain of the Baixo Alentejo, Beja was the Roman city Pax Iulia, founded, according to some scholars, by Julius Caesar, or, according to others, by Augustus. Some remains of the period still survive. Nearby are the ruins of numerous Roman villas including the luxurious farm of Pisões. In Roman times, as now, the area was rich in cereal and livestock production. The soil of the province is littered with Roman pottery, stones, tiles and other fragments and there are scores of potential sites awaiting excavation.

The Visigoths recognized the advantages of the region and the church of Santo Amaro (Beja) preserves some Visigothic columns and capitals. When threatened by Christian advances, the Moslems walled the town of Beja and it remained in their possession until 1162. The castle there was built in the thirteenth century by Dom Denis.

To the east of the capital flows the river Guadiana on its journey southward and beyond it lies the Serra da Adiça along the Spanish border. Southeast is situated the once important city of Mértola with its Roman and Moslem history some of which is laid bare by archaeologists' spades. In the south are the mountains separating Beja from the Algarve and to the southwest the province confronts the Atlantic seaboard.

Évora

The District of Évora, north of Beja, consists of undulating plains, wheat fields, olive trees and vineyards. Essentially a rural area, it is dotted with prehistoric remains (dolmens, menhirs and cromlechs) and Roman villas. The capital city of the Alto Alentejo, Évora, is built on a low hill. It retains its Arabic and Medieval charm, as well as earlier Roman relics including one of the most complete temples in Europe. In Roman times the city, Liberalitas Iulia Ebora, was a place of some importance. In 715 it fell into the hands of the Arabs who called it Yebora (after the original Celtic name) and who held it until 1165.

Within a 25 km radius around Évora are at least 150 megaliths. A guide to these is currently being prepared and will be available at the Turismo office in town. (See also Guadalupe, Montemor-o-Novo, São Brissos, Valverde.)

To the east lies the Serra de Ossa inhabited from prehistoric times as attested by numerous megalithic monuments in the vicinity of Reguengos and Monsaraz. West of Évora is one of the few sites in Portugal with Paleolithic cave paintings: the Grutas do Escoural. Not far away, near Valverde, is the largest dolmen in the country, the Anta do Zambujeiro. To the west, the land rises into the hills of the Serra do Monfurado just south of Montemor-o-Novo.

Faro

The capital city, Faro, lies at the north end of a small sheltered harbour. Paleolithic artifacts, primarily stone tools, have been found in numerous places throughout the region and it is clear that early man inhabited the area, hunting, fishing and collecting shellfish. Archaeological sites have not been as abundant in the Algarve through the Mesolithic, Neolithic and Metal Ages as in many other places but Roman and Moslem remains are more plentiful. The popularity of the southern coast for its climate and scenic beauty has engendered considerable construction of tourist facilities in recent years consisting of new roads, apartment complexes and other establishments detrimental to the preservation of ancient sites. Throughout the past centuries many sites were also obliterated or left in shambles by intensive agricultural production of the fertile earth of the Algarve.

While dolmens, so plentiful in the central and northern sections of the country, are non existent in the Algarve, there are numerous menhirs (few still standing) and some tholoi. Some necropoli, cist graves, from the Bronze Age are known but few have been systematically excavated.

Much of the area may have been under the rule of the legendary Tartessos or Turdetani with whom the Phoenicians made contact perhaps as early as the eighth or seventh century B.C. in their search for metals. A focal point of Phoenicians and later Greeks and Carthaginians, Faro was a trading post of those ancient mariners. Later the Romans made good use of the port. The Visigoths conquered the city in 418, and it was taken by the Arabs in 714. In 1249 the town was captured by the army of Afonso III of Portugal. Some remnants of the Arabic walls, rebuilt in the thirteenth century after the reconquest still remain. Silves was the capital under the Arabs. It was an important river port that carried on trade throughout the Mediterranean. Captured by Christian forces, it was lost and recaptured in 1242 by the Knights of the Order of Santiago. Its importance declined along with the loss of trade with North Africa and the silting up of the river Arade. Lagos was the immediate beneficiary. In classical times, Cabo de São Vicente, the most western area of the Algarve, was the finis terrae of the known world.

The most interesting sites from Roman and Paleo-Christian times are the ruins of Milreu, São Cucufate and those of Vilamoura.

Setúbal

Roman Setúbal, the capital, from the first to the fourth centuries A.D., was an important town primarily involved in fish-curing industries and was served by a conglomerate of these on both sides of the Sado estuary including Tróia. Decline set in with the Germanic invasions and continued through the period of Moslem rule, the latter preferring higher land such as at Palmela and Alcácer do Sal. The Christian conquest of Palmela by Afonso Henriques in 1148 and the subsequent investiture of the city by the Knights of the Order of Santiago, led to the resettlement of Setúbal which was by then overrun by sand dunes.

Once the most powerful stronghold in southern Portugal, the castle, originally Arabic, stands above Palmela. It was taken from the Arabs in the mid-twelfth century, rebuilt, and became the headquarters of the Knights of Santiago. It has undergone many restorations, the last major one in 1940.

The Serra da Arrábida west of the city, where evidence of Lower Paleolithic man has been found in the grotto of Lapa de Santa Margarida, rises above the bay of Setúbal. To the south, across the bay, the land is fairly flat to the Serra de Grándola among whose hills are located the famous Roman ruins of Mirobriga near Santiago do Cacém. To the east, the intermittently hilly countryside around Alcácer do Sal is drained by the river Sado and its tributaries.

SITES AND SIGHTS

BEJA

Aljustrel

The copper, silver, and gold mines were used in Roman times. The deepest level worked by the Romans was 120 m in the Algares bed. The shafts were reached by narrow galleries with niches in the walls for lamps. There is evidence that the mines were worked in Chalcolithic and Bronze Age times dating back to the beginnings of the second millennium B.C. Mining continued down to the fourth or fifth centuries A.D. Excavations of Roman buildings have been disappointing since they were badly ruined but have revealed humble dwellings which may have once housed mine workers. Two bronze tablets, now in the Geological Museum in Lisboa, were found here recording the legislation that governed the mines. To see what is left of the Roman area of the mines permission is required from the company Pirites Alentejaneas S.A. Tel: 084-62106. There is a small museum in situ.

Sight:
Remains of Roman mines.

Location:
Aljustrel lies SW of Beja some 34 km on the N 18/N 2. The mines are above the town in the heart of the industrial mining section.

Almodôvar
Here stands a well-preserved small three-arched Roman bridge.

Sight:
Roman bridge.

Location:
SW of Beja and S of Castro Verde 21 km on the N 2. The bridge is signposted in town.

Baleizão
Excavation of a Roman villa, Herdade de Fonte de Frades. Some sections of the villa were damaged by agricultural machinery but the peristyle, walls,

foundations of structures, remains of baths, mosaics and tanks of various sizes have been found. The site, datable from the first century A.D., was abandoned in the fifth century. It is about 150 m long and can be seen from the road.

Herdade de Montinho, another Roman villa near Baleizão is neglected, overgrown and badly deteriorating. Still to be seen are the remains of interior walls of buildings up to ca. 50 cm high and mosaics which have been left uncovered and are deteriorating from weather and vegetation. There are also the remains of a pool with steps, water conduits, drainage system and various rooms. Reputedly a nearby dam served the villa.

There is also a Roman dam, Monte da Magra, located off the road between Beja and Baleizão.

Near Quintos not far from Baleizão is a Roman villa, Torre da Cardeira, whose plan is only partially understood and which, according to funerary inscriptions, functioned during the second century A.D. It is supposed to have had a dam (not evident) and possibly a temple. It is situated in the rose garden of a farm which adds to its enchantment.

Sights:

Scant remains of two Roman villas: Herdade de Fonte de Frades and Herdade de Montinho. Roman dams.

Remains of Torre da Cardeira, a Roman villa where excavations have revealed foundations of dwellings, baths and other structures whose function is unclear.

Roman villa, Torre de Cardeira, Quintos, Baleizão

Location:

Baleizão is E of Beja 13 km on the N 260. Going toward Beja from Baleizão, after 3.7 km turn left (S) into farm, signposted *Fonte de Frades.* Continue ca. 600 m on unpaved farm road and excavation can be seen on the right. To reach it requires a walk of about 400 m through wheat fields. Ask for Fonte de Frades ruinas romanas.

Herdade de Montinho lies E of Beja. On the N 260, turn right (S) opposite Baleizão at sign *Estação* (RR station). Continue 2.6 km and turn right on farm track opposite house on left. Go 700 km and turn left (or walk) into wheat fields along tractor path and proceed for 200 m to large pile of stones on the right. Excavation is in wheat field to the left ca. 60 m. If lost, ask for Dom Pedro excavation.

For the Roman dam of Monte da Magra, coming from Beja on the N 260, stop just beyond km stone 11. The dam is on the left (N) about 500 m off the road beyond the fields.

Torre da Cardeira lies E of Beja and is most easily reached by turning right off the highway N 260 onto a farm road 1.7 km east of Baleizão. Continue 3 km passing a farm on the right and turn in left at gateposts. Follow this farm track for another 1.3 km to farm and villa. If lost, ask for site by name.

Beja

There is an ongoing excavation of Roman baths in town on the Rua do Sembranhas. The site is currently closed to the public although the city museum has a key to enter. Eventually there should be a museum in situ.

The Roman walls were rebuilt in the Middle Ages and of them today remains only the Porta de Évora which is a Roman arch near the tower of the castle (which was built on the remains of a Roman fortress). The Arco do Avis is another Roman arch in the town wall.

The town of Beja appears to have been founded by the Romans and not built on an existing site as were many other places. Its original name, according to Ptolemy, was Pax Iulia. The forum was where the Praça da República now stands.

Near the town is the large, partially excavated Roman villa of Pisões. The grave goods from the site date from the first century A.D. to the Visigothic period. Unearthed or partially so are about forty rooms centred around a peristyle with four columns and entered by a corridor with rooms off it, one with an apse and pond. The façade of the villa faced south and opened onto a large basin 40 by 8.30 m. In the northwest section were large baths and an open-air swimming pool measuring 6 by 4.6 m. Various rooms and the atrium contain very fine mosaics and decorated walls. The hypocaust has been partially recon-

structed. This particularly wealthy villa was one of several in the vicinity of Beja and follows the plan of other late Roman villas, especially that of Cardílio (Torres Novas). An inscription reveals the name of the family to whom the villa belonged in the first century. Much of this site is yet to be excavated. The remains of a church and cemetery have been protectively re-covered. The site is well maintained and the guard will show visitors around.

Roman villa, Pisões, Beja

Sights:

Roman arches and baths in town. The nearby Roman villa displays remains of rooms, kitchen, corridor, columns, excellent mosaics, baths, swimming pool, hypocaust, fish pond, fountain, well, patios, oil press, graves, nearby dam (200 m).

Location:

Pisões is SW of Beja ca. 10 km. Take the N 10 out of Beja toward Aljustrel but take a right turn before Penedo Gordo and just before a bridge. Follow this unpaved road for 3.7 km to the excavations. They are signposted on the left a short distance from the gate. The dam is on the right, opposite the excavations.

Ferreira do Alentejo

Roman villa Monte da Chaminé, small area excavated. There is not much to see here as yet and much has been destroyed. The mosaics are in a precarious state of preservation and little remains of the interior walls of the rooms and other structures. Coins found here date back to the third and fourth centuries A.D.

Sights:

Roman villa with remnants of hypocaust, columns (not standing) and bases, interior walls of stone and brick, mosaics, millstone.

Location:

W of Beja 23 km on N 121 to Ferreira, then S on the N 2 toward Faro. Go 3.5 km and immediately after bridge crossing the Ribeira da Canhestros, turn right on farm road. Follow this 300 m and excavation is on the right in a wheat field about 100 m from the road. Fenced, after a fashion, but easily accessible.

Marmelar

Vera Cruz de Marmelar is originally a seventh-century church in cruciform style but has undergone restorations. Some of the early constructional elements are still to be seen inside.

Sight:

Visigothic church.

Location:

NE of Beja and SE of Vidigueira 15 km on a secondary road. The church is in the village and key may be obtained at house number 5 next to the school opposite the church.

Mértola

A pre-Roman town during the Bronze and Iron Ages, it was on the road that ran from the estuary of the Tejo and the Sado to that of the lower Guadalquivir. Its Roman name given by Ptolemy (second century A.D.) was Iulia Myrtilis and its importance came from trade and the copper mines at present-day Mina do São Domingos 17 km to the east where the mines were worked from the time of Augustus to that of Theodosius. Of the actual workings there is only an open pit partially filled with water and a narrow, low shaft bored into the side of a hill left to see.

Archaeological work was begun in the city in 1978 around the Roman forum, just below the castle, where at the same time Moslem dwellings were encountered. The site was abandoned during the reconquest and then used as a cemetery during the fourteenth and fifteenth centuries. At the Roman level a cryptoporticus (under the forum), and baths were found, the former used by the Moslems as a cistern. Remains of a temple and basilica were also unearthed and a nearby Roman house has been recently excavated. On the outskirts of town are the remains of the Roman road from Mértola to Beja.

The strategic importance of the town on the Guadiana river continued into the fifth and sixth centuries especially during the short period when southern Lusitania was occupied by Byzantine forces. Many inscriptions from this period have been found. The remains of the walls and floor of a Paleo-Christian basilica in the neighbourhood of Rossio do Carmo and a Visigothic cemetery have also come to light. In the sixth and seventh centuries the town was part of the Visigothic realm. The Early Christian basilica and graves, discovered in 1982, were constructed along the Roman road. The church appears to have fallen into decay in the ninth or tenth century when the area became an Islamic cemetery.

Under Moslem domination the town continued as an important capital up until it was reconquered in 1238 by the Knights of the Order of Santiago.

The Mezquita, a rectangular building in Moslem style, now the Igreja Matriz, underwent profound reparations in the twelfth century during the Almohade dynasty and was remodelled in the sixteenth century by the Christians, but the horseshoe arches of some of the portals and the recently discovered mihrab have survived. Some of the stone and brick work of the southeast portal shows Byzantine influence. Below the town stand the remains of the Torre do Rio on the banks of the Guadiana extending into the river at the end of an offshoot wall from the town ramparts. Here was access to the river and in times of danger a chain could be stretched across the water to impede navigation.

Sights:

Roman and Islamic walls, excavations of the Roman forum, cryptoporticus, baths, water conduits, temple, basilica, road and house. Paleo-Christian basilica (in situ museum is projected), tombs, Moslem castle, Mesquita, Torre do Rio. Artifacts from all epochs are in the Mértola museum.

Location:

Mértola is SE of Beja 50 km on the N 122. All the sights are in and around the town except for the mines at São Domingos which is E of Mértola 17 km on the N 265.

Moura

Roman Arucci and once an important military crossroads. Remains of a Roman bridge and slight traces of a road. There is an Iron Age site, Castro da Azougada ca. 4 km from town but little left to see and difficult access. The castle was constructed on an older Moslem fortification and preserves an Almohade tower. There are also remains of Arabic walls, probably of the eleventh century, but much of the fortifications were rebuilt over centuries and are often difficult to date.

Sights:
Roman bridge and road. Castro. Remains of Arabic castle, walls and tower.

Location:
Moura is NE of Beja on the N 258/N 255. Castle in town. The bridge is on the north side of town over the Ribeira de Brenhas.

Ourique
Luso-Roman settlement or camp, Castro da Cola, by the church of Nossa Senhora da Cola. The site, a rectangular defensive enclosure, is overgrown but interesting. The well cut Roman stone construction is clearly different from the Lusitanian or Celtic section.

Castro da Cola, Ourique

Sights:
Defensive walls, interior dividing wall, cistern with steps, foundations of possible dwellings.

Location:
Ourique is SW of Beja some 60 km. From the town go S on the N 264 toward Faro. Continue past Aldeia dos Palheiros and 9.4 km from Ourique is a sign to the right (W) for Castro da Cola. Travel 4 km to the church and the site is a short walk, on the hill, above.

Selmes
On Monte da Cegonha is a small excavation of a Roman villa of the first to the fourth centuries A.D. with Visigothic and Moslem remains. Little to see at present apart from a few foundations of structures.

Sight:
Remains of a few structures of a Roman villa.

Location:
Selmes is N of Beja. Take the N 18 toward Évora 14 km and turn right (E) after São Matias toward Selmes. Ca. 2 km before Selmes, go right (S) on a difficult rutted farm track to site. Journey not advisable in inclement weather except in an all-terrain vehicle.

Serpa
In Serpa near the Porta de Beja is a large noria, or water wheel, which carried water to the town. Nearby is a neglected Chalcolithic site, Cerro dos Castelos, with a small excavation exposing about 1.5 m of wall on an upper

level and another fragment of wall lower down. This is virtually all there is to see.

There is a Roman dam about 150 m long and 2.5 m high in some places, not far from the city at Monte dos Oliveros, on private land, but accessible. It is constructed of stone and broken in a few places.

In the vicinity are two Roman bridges, both small, one with three arches and heavily overgrown, the second, a humpbacked bridge with six visible arches, lies over the Ribeira do Enxoé.

Sights:

Copper Age settlement remains with fragments of walls. Roman dam. Roman bridges.

Location:

Serpa is SE of Beja 29 km. To reach Cerro dos Castelos, take the road from the public gardens on the S side of town 4.8 km to São Bras and continue through the very small unmarked hamlet on right. Just before the bend in the road and the next farm (Moinhos), and just before the sign to watch out for animals on the road, take the unpaved farm track to the right. Continue 700 m to the top of a knoll where the excavation is on the right.

The Roman dam, Cruz do Sobras, is located E of Serpa along the N 260 ca. 7 km where there is a farm on the left with a large palm tree in front. Go a further 600 m past the farm and turn in left on farm road. Continue 800 m along this track and the dam is on the left.

For the bridges, leave Serpa taking the N 255 (off the N 260) N toward Moura. Proceed only 400 m and the first bridge is on the left, close beside the modern bridge. It is easy to miss from the highway. The second bridge is 8.6 km from the turnoff on the same road to Moura where it also lies to the left of a modern bridge.

Vila de Frades

The Roman villa of São Cucufate, built in the first century A.D., rebuilt in the second century and again in the fourth, has been extensively excavated. It was used as a monastery until the sixteenth century. The monks destroyed some of the outbuildings of the villa and used the space for a cemetery but they preserved the residence which is unique to fourth-century Portugal where the traditional peristyle was favoured. This structure is a rectangular building measuring about 105 by 25 m. The lower floor was used for servants' quarters and storage while the upper storey housed the owner. On the perimeter of the villa stands a temple, similar to the one at Milreu (see Estói), which was adapted to Christian purposes judging from the burials in a gallery around it. The site is not fenced and the visitor may freely inspect the impressive ruins. This is considered to be one of the best preserved Roman monuments in the country.

There are plans for a museum in situ and also for the creation of an archaeological park here.

Sights:

Excavated Roman villa and later monastery. Remains of a temple/church, baths of the second century villa, residence of the fourth century, outbuildings, oil/wine presses, cemetery, terrace, stairs, basin, reservoir at rear.

Roman ruins of São Cucufate, Vila de Frades

Location:

Go N of Beja 27 km on the N 18 to Vidigueira. Turn W on the N 258 toward Vila de Frades. Bypass the town and after the sign for Alvito (some 18 km further W) continue ca. 1.8 km along the road. The ruins are signposted on the right (N) side and can be seen nearby from the road. Turn onto unpaved track to site.

Other sites and sights in the district of Beja include:

Aldeia dos Palheiros

Cist cemetery, overgrown and nearly destroyed with only a few stones left to see. SW of Beja and S of Ourique on the N 264 ca. 7 km. Turn left (E) at restaurant *Coimbra* (just past town). Go up dirt rack to white farmhouse on left. Walk up a further 100 m to olive tree with fence around it. What is left of the cemetery is there.

Alfundão

Small Roman bridge consisting of three spans over a sometime stream on the edge of town. NW of Beja 20 km on the N 121 then 4 km on the N 387 to Peroguarda and a further few km NW to Alfundão.

Alvito

A five-arched powerfully constructed Roman bridge with two smaller arches spanning the river Odivelas. It has been somewhat rebuilt to take modern traffic. Go NW of Beja 27 km on N 18, and W of Vidigueira on the N 258. The bridge lies 2.7 km before reaching Alvito from Vidigueira.

Beringel

Bronze Age site, Outeiro do Circo, with a few vestiges of the ancient settlement as the site has all but disappeared due to ploughing. Overgrown remains of walls. Not much to see.

Beringel is W of Beja on the N 121 toward Lisboa. Travel 11 km from Beja, pass through the village, and go left at the sign for Mombeja. Continue 2.4 km and stop by abandoned farm house on right. Walk up to the top of the hill on the right.

Castro Verde

The industrial area of Neves-Corvo has proven to be very fertile in archaeological finds, especially relating to the Iron Age and the Roman period. In a small area of only 2 square km, for example, four ancient Iron Age villages and two cemeteries have been found. Here also eastern Mediterranean influences are clearly evident, most spectacularly in the form of an engraved stone in the alphabet, so commonly employed in southern Portugal, derived from Graeco-Phoenician sources. These sites are on company property and permission to enter must be obtained from the Neves Corvo company and arranged in advance. The site is SW of Beja 56 km. Go S of Castro Verde toward Almodôvar and turn left (E) S of Rosário at sign for Minas Neves-Corvo, 9 km.

Odivelas

Roman bridge at Caneiras do Roxo. Go W of Beja on the N 121 to Ferreira, then N on the N 2, 13 km.

ÉVORA

Évora

The ancient name of the town, Ebora, appears to have been of Celtic origin suggesting a pre-Roman oppidum on the hill where the present city now stands. Granite blocks, sections of the ancient ramparts remain with square towers, similar to other towns of the Iberian peninsula, and were probably constructed at the beginning of the fourth century A.D. One Roman gate, the Arco de Dona Isabel, is still standing on the north side. Only the outer arch is of this period, the inner one is Medieval and probably dates from the twelfth century. In the Praça do Giraldo stood another Roman arch, demolished in the sixteenth century to expand the church square of Santo Antão.

The Roman temple standing on the summit of the hill in the centre of the city is one of the best preserved on the Iberian peninsula. Often referred to as the Temple of Diana, there seems to be no basis in fact for this designation. It was probably a forum temple dedicated to the Imperial cult. The podium measures 25.18 by 12.25 m. The twenty-eight outer granite columns are fluted and stand 7.68 m high including the fine Corinthian capitals which are 1 m in diameter at the widest point. Dating to the end of the first or beginning of the second century A. D., the temple in Medieval times was employed as a watch tower, later as a building for the Inquisition and finally as a meat market. Only in 1870 was it restored to its present state.

Évora was an important city but contains no other visible ancient remains. The aqueduct, constructed during the reign of João III, is thought to have followed the course of a Roman predecessor whose remains could still be seen in the sixteenth century.

Sights:

Remains of a Roman temple, gate and walls.

Location:

In town.

Guadalupe

Cromlech dos Almendres, an oval-shaped area 60 m by 30 m in which are found 95 prehistoric granite monoliths. Some have spiral engravings.

Nearby is a single, large, upright stone, Menhir dos Almendres 2.5 m high.

Sights:

Cromlech and menhir.

Location:

Take the N 114 from Évora toward Montemor-o-Novo and at 9.5 km turn left to Guadalupe. The cromlech is also signposted here. Continue 7.7 km to site. Well-signposted. The menhir is located in an olive grove behind the grain storage bins of the Co-operativa Agrícola de Agua-de-Lupe which is passed on the left.

Roman temple, Évora

Luz

The fortified Roman villa or fort, Castelo da Lousa, is situated on the river Guadiana. Its plan is rectangular ca. 23 by 20 m with schist walls about 2 m thick, and in some places 5.7 m high. In the centre is a cistern 8 m deep. The rooms with small high windows are arranged around a central courtyard. It was occupied from the first century B.C. to the first century A.D. It may soon be covered by the waters of a dam.

Sight:

Roman fortified villa with remains of walls, cistern.

Location:

SE of Évora. Follow the N 256, 55 km to Mourão then go SW on secondary road to Luz. It is situated on the left bank of the Guadiana but ask in town for Castelo da Lousa.

Cromlech of Almendres, Guadalupe

Montemor-o-Novo

Nearby are the Grutas do Escoural where Paleolithic rupestrian art was discovered accidentally in 1963. The cave is narrow with somewhat steep downward steps at the entrance but the paintings are not far from the entrance. Some fourteen paintings and five engravings have been identified in the cave but many are in a poor state of preservation and barely visible in the best light. Many have been obscured or nearly erased by water or covered over with calcite. Some of them are naturalistic, some semi-schematic and others abstract. These figures of horses, bulls and hybrid animals appear to have been produced between twenty and fifteen thousand years ago.

The cave was also employed as a Neolithic burial ground where the remains of human skeletons, ceramic material and polished stone implements have been unearthed.

On the hill above the cave are the remnants of a Neolithic/Chalcolithic settlement and burials, but little to see. On the hill to the left facing the cave along a heavily overgrown path some 300 m away, are the scant remains of a tholos.

On the road between Évora and Montemor-o-Novo is a dolmen, Anta das Terrais. See also, São Geraldo.

Sights:
Rupestrian paintings and engravings, Neolithic and Chalcolithic necropolis. Dolmen.

Location:
Montemor-o-Novo is W of Évora 30 km on the N 114. Just before the town turn left at the sign for Escoural. Go ca. 12.5 km and the Gruta is signposted on the left just before the quarry. The cave is 3 km from the village of Santiago do Escoural. Hours are posted 9-12 and 1:30-5 except Mondays but it is not

Megalithic tomb and chapel, Pavia

always open at the times stated. Guard on duty.

The Anta das Terrais is on the N 114 going W from Évora and is ca. 6 km before Montemor-o-Novo on the left. Opposite, on the right, is a farm house with a large tower.

Pavia

Megalithic tomb whimsically encompassing within the confines of its burial chamber a tiny chapel which contains a blue-tiled altar and statue of the Virgin.

Sight:
Unusual megalithic tomb with chapel inside.

Location:

Pavia is on the N 251 NW of Évora and 40 km W of Estremoz. The mega-lith/chapel is in town on the top of the hill. The key is obtainable at the *Café Dolmen* beside it.

Reguengos de Monsaraz

The municipality of Reguengos is one of the richest in the country for megalithic remains including rare enclosures such as the one at Xeres and phallic menhirs of Bulhôa and Outeiro. The region appears to have been the home of cults practising intensive fertility rites.

The well-preserved Cromlech do Xerez, consists of a vertical stone or menhir, 4 m high, weighing about 7 tons, and surrounded by a circle of 52 smaller standing stones or little menhirs, many of which are fractured, some have phallic characteristics. The large menhir is decorated at the base with some faint lines of reputed fertility symbols.

The Menhir de Bulhôa stands alone. It had fallen over and was broken but has been patched to-gether and set upright. The base of the column, once used as a mill-stone, was destroyed and a new one was constructed from granite in 1970. The menhir is about 4 m high and shows some engravings on two sides consisting of zigzags, a sun and other curvilinear configurations (difficult to see). About 50 m south-east are the remnants of a ruined dolmen.

Nearby stands the 5.6 m-tall, 8 ton, Menhir de Outeiro which also had fallen and was set upright in 1969 and has an engraving at the top of a masculine meatus of the ure-thra.

Not far away are the Antas do Olival da Pega dating back to about 3000 B.C. Anta II, under excavation, has a huge capstone but the cham-ber is currently filled with broken stones. The passageway is partially excavated. Situated close by is an-other very large dolmen, Anta I, on

Menhir of Bulhôa, Reguengos

the opposite side of the road among a cluster of olive trees, with several huge standing chamber stones but no capstone. Many other stones including those of the passageway have fallen over. After the dolmen of Zambujeiro (Évora) this is perhaps the second largest in the country.

The so-called Menhir da Rocha dos Namorados is a tall natural rock worn away by erosion, recognizable by the many small stones on the top, thrown there over the shoulders of young ladies who, as legend has it, can count the number of years before marriage by the number of times it takes to place a stone on the top. This ancient pagan fertility rite is practised by the local girls on Easter Monday.

Sights:

Dolmens, menhirs and cromlechs.

Location:

Reguengos is SE of Évora 35 km. Take the N 256 toward Mourão to the E and turn off left (N) for Monsaraz (14 km beyond Reguengos). Continue for 3 km to where there is a farm and sign *Xerez* on the right. Continue 50 m further along the road and turn left onto unpaved track. Go 300 m to gate, Menhir and Cromlech on the right beside the farm road.

For Bulhôa and Outeiro continue up to and just beyond Monsaraz and at T junction turn right and follow the road down to Telheiro. Where road curves left, take right fork into town and go right on road toward Outeiro. Go 900 m and pass over small bridge. The Menhir of Bulhôa is on the left about 200 m off the road.

Continue on the same road another 1 km to T junction in the village and turn left. About 900 m further is a small blue-and-white church. There is a small sign *Menhir*. Turn right passing behind the church and continue along the heavily rutted farm track (not advisable in inclement weather due to the glutinous texture of the mud) a little over 800 m to site of Outeiro in a field on the left.

The Antas do Olival da Pega are reached by continuing from Telheiros toward Reguengos W, turnoff right 2.2 km onto gravel road. Stop after 300 m where there is a sign *Anta II* and walk ca. 100 m to dolmen straight ahead. The other dolmen can be found by continuing 200 m down the gravel road where it is about 50 m off the road to the left in some olive trees, but is not signposted.

Menhir and cromlech of Xerez, Reguengos

Continuing W on the road toward Reguengos 6.9 km and 500 m before the village of São Pedro de Corval (5.5 km before Reguengos) stands the Menhir dos Namorados on the right. (There is a football field on the left.)

At the time of writing there are no access roads into the Menhir das Vidigueiras or the megalithic monument of Recinto da Farizoa mentioned in tourist brochures and local maps. Similarly, the Cromlech da Capela, now reduced to four broken stones, and the Menhir dos Perdigões, with seven stones mostly broken, situated 2 km N of Reguengos, are not accessible by road.

The Turismo office in Reguengos will provide further updated information.

São Brissos, dolmen/chapel

Santa Vitoria do Ameixial

Fenced, partially excavated Roman villa with remains of a few dwellings and some walls. Excavated in 1915 and 1916, there is now little left. This was once a very rich villa judging from the mosaics, one of which depicts one of Ulysses' ships by the island of the Sirens. Unfortunately, the site has largely been destroyed by the building of houses over it using its materials in their construction.

Sights:
Remnants of a Roman villa.

Location:
Santa Vitoria is NE of Évora and NW of Estremoz off the N 245. Take road into town and at other end of the town the site is on the right.

São Brissos

The Anta do São Brissos is a chapel grafted onto a dolmen uniting Christianity with the Neolithic. It stands alone in a remote field. Unfortunately, the dolmen, with its large capstone, has been whitewashed to match the chapel with disappointing results.

Sight:
Dolmen/chapel.

Location:
W of Évora, take the N 380 toward Alcáçovas. Pass Valverde and go 11 km more, past Brissos, to the hermitage of Nossa Senhora do Livramento. The tiny church/dolmen is on the left side of the road and signposted.

São Geraldo

Large dolmen referred to as the Anta Grande da Comenda da Igreja. It is in a reasonably good state of preservation with capstone in place.

Sight:
Dolmen.

Location:

Take the N 2, N from Montemor-o-Novo to just before São Geraldo, and the dolmen is signposted to the left. It stands about 500 m from the road.

Valverde

The Anta do Zambujeiro nearby is of a massive size, reputedly the largest dolmen on the Iberian peninsula. The entrance passage, with some stones askew, is about 14 m long. The upright chamber stones, up to 6 m high, and capstone are of enormous dimensions. The artifacts from the tomb are in the Museum of Évora.

Excavation of another dolmen is currently taking place near Valverde, but to date it is not open to the public.

Sight:

Extremely large dolmen.

Location:

SW of Évora. Follow the N 380 toward Alcáçovas ca. 10 km to turnoff for Valverde. The dolmen is then signposted by a large farm in the village. Go

Anta do Zambujeiro, Valverde

through the farm gate and take left fork following the dirt road for 1.1 km which leads up to the top of a gentle hill, descends slightly and passes over a small bridge. The dolmen is just ahead.

Other sites and sights in the district of Évora include:

Aldeia da Serra

Anta da Candeeira. An easy dolmen to find about 200 m from the road. Anyone in the village will point it out. NE of Évora 45 km. Go S of Estremoz ca. 17 km on the N 381 to Aldeia da Serra.

Nossa Senhora da Torega

Remains of a Roman villa with foundations of structures. Mosaics were also discovered here. SW of Évora ca. 10 km. The ruins are near the church cemetery. There is also a reputed Bronze Age oppidum and cemetery nearby.

FARO

Abicada

Roman villa partially excavated in 1938. Now several kilometres from the sea, the villa was once on the coast and could accommodate ships to transport its products. The site is easily accessible but fenced. The guard will appear and unlock the gate. A large part is either destroyed or re-covered except for the main area paved with mosaics, some of which are under sand for preservation. Coins found at the site range from the first to the fourth centuries A.D.

Roman villa of Abicada

Sights:

Roman villa with mosaics, foundations of about two dozen rooms, two atria or small peristyles (hexagonal and rectangular), fish salting tanks about 20 m to the SW.

Location:

W of Faro. Take the N 125 just beyond Portimão, after exit for Alvor. At the sign on the right (N) for Figueira, go left (S) into small village. This is Abicada (not marked). Go to T junction, ca. 100 m, and turn right 50 m taking first left. Continue along unpaved roadway across RR track and take the right fork through property of Aquazul S.A. Continue to the end of the road and farmhouse which is adjacent to the excavation. (Ca. 9 km from Portimão).

Alamo

Small Roman dam, Barragem Romana do Alamo, alongside the road but hidden from view in the trees and bushes. About 90 metres away from the dam are the remnants of a Roman villa, somewhat excavated, but of which little remains. Traces of a Paleo-Christian basilica of the fifth and sixth centuries have been reported.

Sights:

Roman dam of earth and stone. Slight remains of Roman villa.

Location:

Alamo is NE of Faro across the river from the Spanish border. Enter Alamo from Alcoutim by following the road south along the river Guadiana. Pass over a small bridge and there is a well on the left (E). 20 m to the right of the road is the dam. (0.8 km from Guerreiros do Rio).

Alcalar

Necrópole do Alcalar of the third millennium B.C. is situated on the summit of a hillock. Excavations have exposed the narrow entranceway of ca. 8 m long and 38 cm wide, and the burial chamber, about 2 m in diameter. The Chalcolithic site is unprotected, neglected and deteriorating.

Sight:

Tholos type grave with chamber and corridor.

Location:

The site lies W of Faro. Turn right (N) off the N 125 at sign for Alcalar (W of Portimão) and follow the road 4 km to village of Alcalar (at split take left fork over small bridge and then under RR arch). Continue 600 m beyond village to crossroad and turn right onto dirt track for 50 m. Walk up left through gate ca. 100 m to top of gentle slope.

Necropolis of Alcalar

Alcoutim

In town stands a Medieval castle greatly rebuilt in the fourteenth century. From it can be seen the ruins of the Castelo Velho or old castle on a hilltop called the Cerro da Mina, about 2 km away. Excavation of the interior of the old castle has revealed rooms and corridors some with remains of walls standing about 5 m high. The views from the ramparts over the river Guadiana of an area blanketed with wild flowers is nothing short of spectacular.

Sight:

The remains of the old castle of Alcoutim.

Location:

NE of Faro and just across the river Guadiana from the Spanish border on the N 122-1. Leaving Alcoutim northward, cross the bridge and continue about 400 m to sign on the right *Pousada de Juventud*. Turn right and continue past the Pousada ca. 800 m to where the road forks. Take the left fork, go up around the bend in the road about 100 m and climb up the hill on the left for about 50 m through prickly bushes.

Budens

Roman villa, Boca do Rio, partially excavated in the 1870s revealed baths, mosaics, wall paintings and fish-salting tanks, and a hoard of a thousand coins, but little can be seen today. Parts of this neglected but once wealthy villa have collapsed onto the beach and sections of wall can be found there. The site is fenced, but the fence, like the villa, is eroding.

Sights:
Scant remains of a Roman villa with remnants of baths and interior walls.

Location:
W of Faro and W of Lagos some 20 km on the N 125 toward Sagres. Turn left (S) toward the sea opposite sign for entrance to Budens. Follow the unpaved road ca. 3 km to the beach just before which the road splits. Take the left fork and the excavation is on the right adjacent to and facing the sea.

Estói
The Roman villa of Milreu is one of the largest villas in the country; it was first excavated in 1877, but part of the structures were re-covered. There remains, however, a good deal to see of this site occupied in the first or second century A.D. and then extensively rebuilt in the fourth.

The villa was constructed around a peristyle of twenty-two columns. One large room has an apse and may have been a kitchen. Near this were the baths with a large dressing room and a circular pool. One of the baths is decorated with brightly coloured mosaics of fish. On the east side of the peristyle the private rooms of the villa were situated around an atrium.

There are also the remains of a temple dedicated to aquatic divinities. The podium was covered with mosaics of fish and dolphin, and it had a square cella ending in an apse. Constructed about the beginning of the fourth century A.D., the temple is similar to that of São Cucufate (Vila de Frades). A little later, perhaps in the fifth century, it was converted into a church and in the sixth or seventh century a baptistry was built within the walled enclosure.

An eighteenth century building was erected on the eastern part of the villa under which recent excavations have revealed a second Roman bath.

Roman bath, Milreu, Estói

Various excavated sections of the villa which are most prominent date back to the third, fourth and sixth centuries and may be individually identified by recourse to the information brochures at the gate, printed in several languages.

Sights:
Late Roman villa with peristyle, atrium, gallery, kitchen, walls, rooms, baths, apodyterium (dressing room), cold, tepid and hot water pools, poly-

chrome floor and wall mosaics, street, entrance, baptismal pool, basin, temple, cella, apse.

Location:

N of Faro ca. 8 km on the N 2 to Coira da Burra where *ruinas* and Estói are signposted on the right. After taking this turnoff, the ruins are on the left, 500 m. Fenced, but open at regular hours.

Montinho das Laranjeiras

A Roman villa explored in 1877. The site was later used as a cemetery which destroyed much of the remains. There is now little left to see except the scant foundations of a few rooms.

Sights:

Slight remains of a Roman villa.

Location:

NE of Faro and S of Alcoutim. Taking the road from Alcoutim travel ca. 10 km along the river Guadiana and just before entering the village of Montinho, the site is on the left (E, toward the river), just before the bridge.

Sagres

Roman fourth century excavated site, Ruinas do Martinhal (or Murtinhal), with the remains of three kilns, and a possible fourth, for the production of pottery (including amphoras), spreads along the beach cliff for about 150 m. Through neglect and erosion there is not much left to see. Most of the remains of the ovens have disappeared into the sea. Soon there will be nothing left.

Sight:

Roman kilns.

Location:

W of Faro. Just before entering Sagres, take the left turn 1 km to Praia de Martinhal. Follow the old road right, and just past the motel go right on sandy track down toward the beach and cliff. Excavation is on the left along the edge of the cliff.

Santa Justa

Hilltop Chalcolithic fortified settlement of Santa Justa. There is little left for the visitor to see here except some of the walls and a great accumulation of stones where they have collapsed.

Sight:

Slight remains of a Copper Age fortified settlement.

Location:

NE of Faro. Take the N 2/N124 to Martim Longo and turn off right (S) on road toward Vaqueiros. At fork take road left to Santa Justa and in the village ask for ruinas. Requires some uphill walking.

Silves

Well-preserved, large Arabic castle, Castelo dos Mouros, with crenellated battlements of red sandstone overlooking the town. On the northern side are some vestiges of the palace of Aben Afan, the last of the Arabic kings of Silves. Within the walls is a vaulted cistern, or well, with stairs, reaching a depth of about 10 m along with underground silos. Silves was once the capital of the Moslem kingdom of the Algarve. The castle appears to have been constructed on earlier Roman fortifications prior to which there may have been a Phoenician stronghold. The thirteenth century bridge in town is said to have been built on the site of a Roman bridge.

The Municipal Museum of Archaeology contains an in situ Moslem (Almohade) well, stairs and section of wall.

Sights:

Arabic castle and cisterns, stairs and wall.

Location:

Silves is ca. 57 km W of Faro and 14.5 km N of Portimão.

Moorish castle, Silves

Vila do Bispo

Three small sandstone menhirs, Menires da Pedra Escorregadia, lying down, the largest about 2 m long. They date from the end of the Neolithic period or from the fourth to the third millennium B.C. Little to see.

Sights:

Three fallen menhirs.

Location:

Vila do Bispo is W of Faro and 26 km W of Lagos. Go out of town (S) on the N 268 toward Sagres. After about 1 km there is a house on the left and turn into pathway left opposite next house on the right. Walk up dirt path to top of knoll.

Vilamoura

The Roman villa, Cerro da Vila (Quarteira), one of the richest in the country, flourished during the first to the fifth century A.D. under Roman ownership, from the fifth to the eighth century under the Visigoths, and from the eighth until at least the tenth under the Arabs. A large part of the walls were destroyed in the 1960s. Systematic excavation began in 1971 although as late as 1963 fragments of mosaics were still being ripped up by farm machinery and discarded, and stones (that hindered cultivation) carried away. During the eight hundred years of occupation, the buildings on the site were rebuilt many times. This fact, coupled with vandalism and agricultural destruction, has left many unsolved problems concerning the exact nature and layout of the site.

The flat land here is very fertile and the existence of a lagoon in which a harbour was constructed in Roman times facilitated shipment of products.

A dam has been identified at Vale Tesnado, nearly 2 km to the northeast, with remnants of an aqueduct 1700 m long to carry water to the villa.

The most distinctive structures so far excavated include the Casa dos Mosaicos, a grand house of mosaics and baths, and one of the oldest uncovered, the ruins of the Balneário Grande, the largest building at Cerro da Vila, with a large heated room, a large cold water swimming pool with steps, and a spacious area that was once a cistern. There are also several sets of baths with caldarium, tepidarium and frigidarium and associated pipes and water conduits. The Casa Pequena, also containing mosaics, appears to have been used for industrial or agricultural purposes. Nearby is an important system of pipes and water tanks that may have been used to treat the water for the Balneário Grande. Other tanks point to the production of garum.

The villa had its own harbour or dock complex which may be seen on the south side toward the sea but this is not completely excavated. There is an extensive cemetery on the north side.

Visigothic and Arabic artifacts attest to the continued occupation of the site.

Sights:

Well-maintained villa. Remains of dwellings, rooms and workshops, traces of walls with painted plaster, exedra, some reset columns and pedestals, mosaics, baths, pools, steps, fountains, pipes or water conduits, garum tanks, under-floor heating system (hypocaust), remains of a columbarium, cemetery, wharf, silos and partially excavated cryptoporticus.

Some Bronze Age stone graves have been brought to the site from several kilometres away and reassembled. They are near the main entrance.

Museum in situ which has a map of some other minor Roman sites in the area.

Locations:

The site is W of Faro some 20 km and on the coast. From the N 125 going W take the turn into Vilamoura and follow it down toward the marina. Turn right after Galp petrol station. The site, about 2 km from the village of Quarteira, is on the right, signposted *Estação Arqueológico*. It lies 400 m from the coast and is near the NW corner of the new marina.

Roman villa, Cerro da Vila, Vilamoura

Other sites and sights in the district of Faro include:

Albufeira

Ruins of an Arabic castle. The name derives from Arabic Al-Buhera or Castle-on-the-sea. On the coast, a little W of Faro.

Aljezur

Bronze Age cist graves, Corte Cabreira, and the remains of an Arabic castle above the town. The castle was devastated by the earthquake of 1755. The graves are neglected, overgrown, many destroyed and difficult to find. Aljezur is NW of Faro and NW of Lagos near the west coast on the N 120. The castle is in town but the Bronze Age necropolis lies some 7 to 8 km up a forestry trail on top of a mountain. The road is steep and difficult at the best of times and impassable in inclement weather. It is best to inquire at the Câmara Municipal for directions and conditions as it is easy to get lost up there.

Of the fifty or so recorded sites of archaeological interest in the municipality, ranging from Paleolithic to Medieval times, all, with few exceptions, are either destroyed or close to it.

Castro Marim

Situated on the banks of the Guadiana river and once an ancient crossroads there are nearby remnants of the Roman road to Mértola. Numerous Roman architectural remains have been found around the thirteenth century castle but little left to see now. NE of Faro and 4 km N of Vila Real de Santo António on the Spanish border.

Conceição

Roman bridge. NE of Faro and 8 km E of Tavira. Take road left (N). Bridge is 700 m off the road.

Ferragudo

Reputed remains of a Roman villa with mosaics and fish salting tanks on the castle grounds. The castle is generally open only a few months in the summer. Ferragudo is W of Faro and SW of Lagoa, ca. 8 km.

Lagos

A large Roman dam, Fonte Coberta, located in the Bairro da Abrotéa. Difficult to find but the museum in Lagos will give detailed directions. Lagos is W of Faro some 71 km on the coast.

Loulé

Roman bridge, Ponte de Tôr, located in Loulé 25 km NW of Faro and may be seen from the N 270 just before the turn off N toward Tôr when travelling E. The castle, rebuilt in the thirteenth century, may be of Arabic origins as are the ramparts.

Paderne

Reputed remnants of a Roman road E of the town and near the castle. NW of Faro and NNE of Albufeira on the N 395 ca. 12 km.

Salir

Vestiges of an Arabic castle NW of Faro and 16 km N of Loulé on the N 124.

São Bras de Alportel

Nearby remains of a Roman road and bridge at Hortas e Moínhos. São Bras de Alportel is N of Faro 17 km on the EN 2. The site is ca. 1 km south of São Bras.

Tavira

The bridge here was once part of the Roman road from Faro to Mértola but was rebuilt in the seventeenth century. About 7 km SW near Torre de Ares on the coast is a Medieval watchtower. Tavira is a coastal resort town NE of Faro some 30 km on the N 125.

Vila Nova de Cacela

There are some reputed remains of strong walls and fish salting tanks from the Roman period in the vicinity of the church and the fort, and a Roman dam over the river Hortinha. E of Faro and about 10 km E of Tavira off the N 125.

SETÚBAL

Alcácer do Sal

The castle on the hill above the town and the river Sado was constructed in Moslem times, was partially rebuilt, but is now mostly in ruins. It fell to Christian forces in 1158, fell back into Moslem hands under the Almohades in 1191 and was again retaken in 1217 with the help of a contingent of crusaders who had anchored their ships in the estuary.

Next to the castle is a partial excavation of the Roman town, Urbs Salacia Imperatoria (the name based on the salt marshes below the town), which appears to have been built on an earlier Iron Age settlement. The pre-Roman burial site, sometimes mentioned in guidebooks, has disappeared under recent building.

Sights:

Small excavation of Roman remains with a few foundations of structures but little to see. Ruined Moslem castle.

Location:

Alcácer do Sal is SE of Setúbal 50 km on the N 5/E 01. The castle is signposted in town and the excavation is adjacent to the road (on left) descending from the castle gate.

Quinto do Anjo

Burial chambers cut from a small rocky knoll, with manhole covers. They were used about 3500 B.C. and continued as sepulchres for about one thousand years, that is, from the Neolithic to the beginning of the Chalcolithic period. Taken from the tombs during the two explorations in 1876 and 1907 were objects of personal and religious use such as arms, ornaments, ceramics, and figurines placed next to the bodies. Among the great variety of grave goods were Bell Beaker (campaniforme) ceramics decorated with geometric designs. The site is open (no fence) and neglected but of no small interest for the period.

Sights:

Prehistoric burial chambers.

Location:

NW of Setúbal and W of Palmela ca. 3.5 km on the N 379 road out of town passing the Turismo office. After entering Quinto do Anjo, turn left at cross-roads in the centre of the town. Continue up this road (slight incline) toward the hill and the sign *Grutas*. Burial chambers are ca. 800 m from the crossroad.

Santiago do Cacém

The likely Roman name of the ancient city nearby was Mirobriga Celticum. The ruins have been of interest since the sixteenth century but systematic excavations only began in the 1940s.

Pre-Roman occupation of the site extends back to the ninth or eighth century B.C. and in the fifth and fourth centuries there was an Iron Age fortified settlement here.

The Roman city which developed did not have a regular street plan because of the difficult sloping topography. Traces of the defensive wall have been found. An area, paved in marble at the top of the slope and dominated by a small temple, could have been the forum. On the southeast side of it, following the slope, a large building was constructed whose walls still stand about 10 m high. It was divided into various tabernae or shops and was undoubtedly commercial premises. Steps through it gave access from the compound or forum to the road. Nearby, also, are structures with wall murals.

Prehistoric burial chamber, Quinto do Anjo

Along the main street, which visitors now take, are the remains of small houses and shops. In the lower part of the city were the baths dating back to the first century A.D. In the second century further baths were built adjacent to the earlier ones and these remain today the best preserved Roman baths in the country, retaining two complete hypocausts, nearly complete pavements, marble baths and walls still standing up to the height of the windows. About 1 km from the centre of the city toward the south is the circus or hippodrome but there is little to see from ground level. When and why the city was abandoned is not known but decoration on a capital indicates its survival at least up to the Visigothic epoch. Artifacts from here are on display in the Santiago do Cacém municipal museum.

The site is open during normal hours and closed on Mondays and holidays.

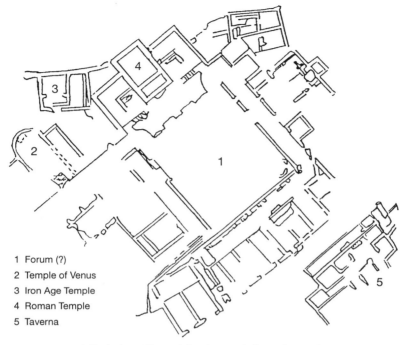

1 Forum (?)
2 Temple of Venus
3 Iron Age Temple
4 Roman Temple
5 Taverna

Mirobriga: Plan of the forum (after Alarcão)

The castle in town is said to be Arabic but it was rebuilt by the Knights Templar.

Sights:

Ruins of Mirobriga, Roman oppidum. Remains of forum, temple, paved roadways, mosaics, columns, steps, dwellings, commercial premises, wall paintings, east and west baths including entranceways, hypocausts, latrines, cold, tepid and hot water pools. Small bridge over a stream on the road to the hippodrome.

Location:

S of Setúbal ca. 70 km. Mirobriga is just off the road toward Lisboa going N out of town. Signposted on the right ca. 1 km.

Torrão

Chalcolithic site, Monte da Tumba, south of Torrão on a small hill offering a good defensive position and accessible water at the confluence of two streams. Excavations were initiated in 1982 when the construction of a house was begun on the site. The first settlement consisted of a defensive wall around a small enclosure and contained silos or storage pits and dates back to about 2500 B.C. Later a second defensive wall was constructed about 1.5 m thick and close to 2 m high. The final stage of occupation of the site appears to have been sometime around the close of the third millennium B.C. There are remains of circular towers and semicircular battlements.

The site is fenced and a small museum has been proposed.

Roman city of Mirobriga, partial view

Sights:

Copper Age site, two defensive walls, remains of round stone houses and towers. Some reconstruction.

Location:

Torrão is SE of Setúbal and 35 km E of Alcácer do Sal on the N 5. The site lies S of Torrão and slightly west 1200 m on a knoll. Ask for Monte da Tumba.

Tróia

Roman fishing settlement situated on the water's edge whose chief industry appears to have been the production of garum and cured fish. It seems to have developed in the first century A.D. A report written in 1858 describes fish salting tanks extending 4 km along the shores of the Sado river. The Latin name of the site is unclear.

Of the buildings discovered in the nineteenth century—baths, an Early Christian chapel, a columbarium and a baptistry—only the latter has disappeared once

Tróia, fish-curing vats

again under the sand dunes. In the southern part of the excavated town is a late Roman or Early Christian cemetery of the fourth or fifth century A.D. but there is little now to see. It is not clear why the city was abandoned.

This well-maintained site is fenced but the guard will open the gate for visitors.

Sights:

Remains of houses, baths, columbarium, many large garum vats, early chapel, coffins, streets.

Location:

Tróia is S of Setúbal across the Sado estuary. Coming from Alcácer do Sal take the N 253 ca. 29 km to Comporta. Go N along the promontory about 15 km and 2.5 km before Tróia, a sign states *Ruinas Romanas.* (If coming the other way from Setúbal, the sign cannot be seen!). Turn in right (E) and the ruins are on the right near the water, 2.8 km at the end of the unpaved track.

Other sites and sights in the district of Setúbal include:

Palmela

Arabic castle originally and remains of a Roman road behind and below the castle. Palmela is N of Setúbal ca. 9 km on the motorway toward Lisboa. The castle is signposted in town.

Sesimbra

A minor road leads SW from the town to the restored Castle of Sesimbra of Arabic origin. Excellent views of the coast. In the vicinity is a prehistoric cave but nothing left to see. Sesimbra is SW of Setúbal ca. 27 km on the N 379.

SUGGESTED ROUTES

NORTHERN PORTUGAL

1. From Penafiel
(1) Oldrões (Monte Mozinho), (2) São Vicente de Pinheiro (Luso-Roman baths), (3) Boelhe (church of São Gens), (4) Luzim (petroglyphs), (5) Santa Marta (dolmen).

2. From Porto
(1) Ovil (dolmen), (2) Baião (dolmens), (3) Marco de Canaveses (Roman town).

3. From Viseu
(1) Mangualde (Citânia, graves, dolmen), (2) Bodiosa (dolmens), (3) Bodiosa-a-Velha (Roman road), (4) São Pedro do Sul (Roman baths, Bronze Age rock carving), (5) Fataunços (Roman bridge and road), (6) Carvalhais (castro).

4. From Viseu
(1) Almargem (Bigas) (Roman road), (2) Lamas (rupestrian inscriptions), (3) São Pedro de Balsemão (seventh century church).

CENTRAL PORTUGAL

5. From Lisboa
(1) Vila Franca de Xira (anthropomorphic tombs), (2) Torres Vedras (Castro de Zambujal), (3) Odrinhas (Roman villa, Cromlech da Barreira), (4) Cheleiros (Roman bridge), (5) Sintra (Castelo dos Mouros).

6. From Lisboa
(1) Leceia (Copper Age settlement), (2) Abóbada (Roman villa), (3) Alapraia (Copper Age burial chambers), (4) Casais Velhas (Roman villa), (5) Almoçageme (Roman villa), (6) Sintra (Castelo dos Mouros).

7. From Castelo de Vide
(1) Anta da Melriça (dolmen), (2) Anta do Alcogulo (dolmen), (3) Anta do Sobral (dolmen), (4) Necrópole de Sto. Amarinho (Visigothic cemetery, chafurdão), (5) Antas dos Coureleiros (dolmens), (6) Necrópole de Azinhaga da Boa Morte (Medieval cemetery) (7) Mosteiros (Roman kiln, dolmen), (8) Anta de São Gens (dolmen, anthropomorphic tombs).

8. From Marvão

(1) Menhir da Agua de Cuba (menhir), (2) Vidais (Roman wine presses, Bronze Age settlement, dolmens), (3) Dolmen da Bola de Cera (dolmen), (4) Anta dos Pombais (dolmen), (5) São Gens (Bronze Age settlement), (6) Vale do Cano (rock-cut tombs and wine press).

SOUTHERN PORTUGAL

9. From Évora

(1) Anta do Zambujeiro (dolmen), (2) Anta do São Brissos (dolmen/chapel), (3) Grutas do Escoural (Paleolithic rupestrian art), (4) Anta das Terrais (dolmen), (5) Guadalupe (cromlech, menhir), (6) Pavia (dolmen/chapel), (7) Anta Grande da Comenda da Igreja (dolmen).

10. From Reguengos

(1) Cromlech do Xerez (cromlech and menhir), (2) Menhir de Bulhôa (menhir), (3) Menhir de Outeiro (menhir), (4) Antas do Olival da Pega (dolmens), (5) Menhir dos Namorados (menhir), (6) Recinto da Farizoa (cromlech), (7) Menhir das Vidigueiras (menhir).

11. From Faro

(1) Estói (Roman villa), (2) Vilamoura (Roman villa), (3) Silves (Moorish castle), (4) Abicada (Roman villa), (5) Alcalar (Copper Age necropolis), (6) Budens (Roman remains), (7) Vila do Bispo (menhirs).

Route 1. from Penafiel

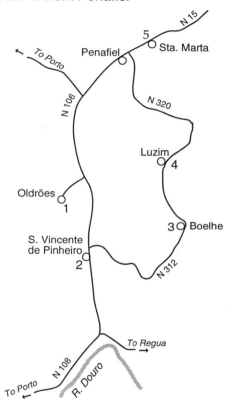

Route 2. from Porto

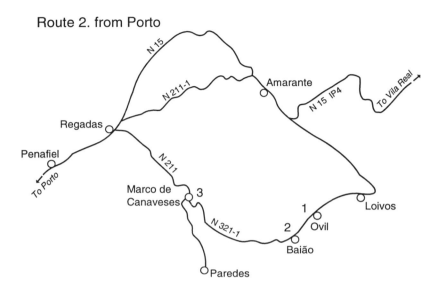

Route 3. from Viseu

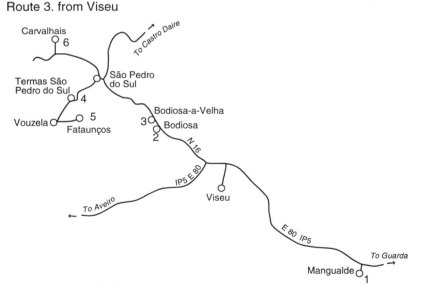

Route 4. from Viseu

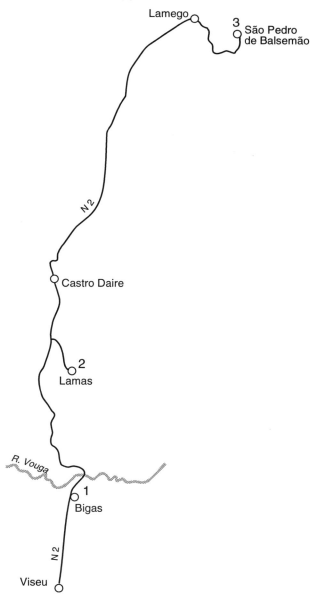

Lamego

3 São Pedro
de Balsemão

N 2

Castro Daire

2
Lamas

R. Vouga

1
Bigas

N 2

Viseu

Route 5. from Lisboa

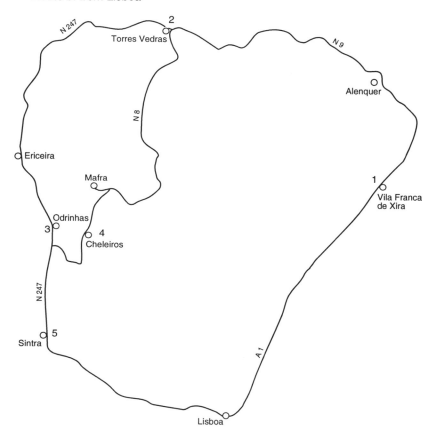

Route 6. from Lisboa

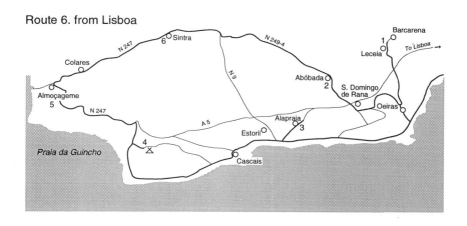

Route 7. from Castelo de Vide

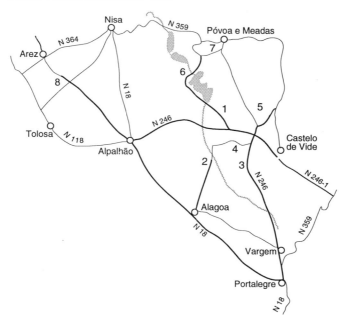

Route 8. from Marvão

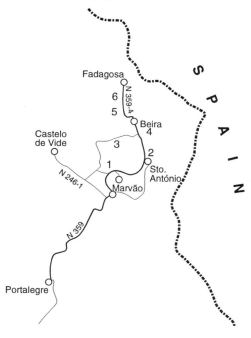

Route 9. from Évora

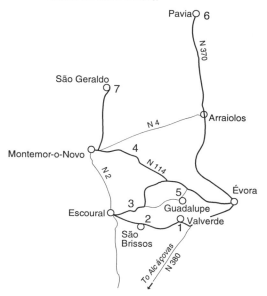

Route 10. from Reguengos

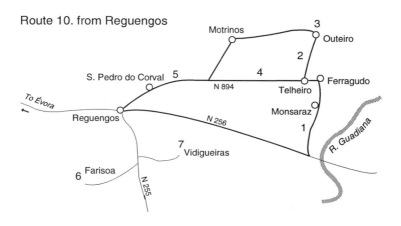

Route 11. from Faro

Glossary

A guide to terms found in this text and those employed at ancient sites to denote various sights.

ajimece	Moorish window of two parts divided by a narrow column
alcáçar	fortress, castle, royal palace
amphora	ceramic receptacle, usually large
anta	megalithic collective tomb normally composed of a chamber and corridor. Also called **dolmen** and **orca**
anthropomorphic	in the shape of a human being
apodyterium	dressing room
ara	votive or funerary altar
atrium	main living room of a Roman villa with an opening in the roof and usually a small fountain or pool below
balneario	baths
barragem	dam
basilica	public building in Roman times that served as a court of justice, reunions and exchange
Bell Beaker	a drinking vessel associated with Copper and Bronze Age peoples
calçada	road
caldarium	hot room of Roman baths
Câmara Municipal	Town Hall
campaniforme	highly decorated type of pottery shaped like an inverted bell appearing in the last phase of the Chalcolithic period
capela	chapel
Cardial Ware	(also known as **Impressed Ware**) type of decorated pottery associated with Neolithic peoples
cardo maximus	a major artery of a Roman city running north-south; the parallel streets were the **cardines minores**

castelo	castle
castro	Celtic or Roman hill fort
cella	main room of a temple, containing an image of a deity
chafurdão	stone circular building with roof of straw, whose origins are uncertain
Chalcolithic	Copper Age
cist grave	box-shaped burial structures of stone slabs set on edge and placed below ground or on the surface, covered by a protective mound
citânia	ancient city
civitas	Roman territorial unit, surrounding an administrative centre
columbarium	Roman grave usually built up above ground with niches for urns in the walls
concelho	municipality
corbelling	a technique for roofing stone chambers
corniche	a roadway or path cut into the side of a steep slope
cromlech	circle of monoliths which are often set on edge in the ground
cryptoporticus	in Roman architecture a gallery, wholly or partially concealed, with few openings
curia	room or building for the meetings of the city council
decumanus maximus	a major artery of a city running east-west; parallel streets were the **decumani minores**
dolmen	a type of collective tomb (see **anta**)
domus	wealthy, urban house
enceinte	enclosure of a castle wall
estação	station
estrada	road (see also **calçada**)
excavações	excavations
ex voto	religious offering
forum	the political, economic, judicial and religious centre of a Roman city, usually situated at the crossing of the Cardo Maximus and Decumanus Maxiumus
freguesia	parish
frigidarium	cold room in Roman baths
garum	sauce of salted fish and fishparts stirred in vats and exposed to the heat of the sun
granja	farm

Hallstatt	designation of a group of communities practising iron metallurgy whose influence spread throughout Europe in the fifth century B.C.
herdade	farm property, estate
hypocaust	Roman under-the-floor central heating system
Idade do Bronze	Bronze Age
igreja	church
impluvium	cistern or tank in the atrium of a Roman house
in situ	at the site
Judiaria	Jewish quarter
Magdalenense	culture of the Upper Paleolithic
mamoa	semicircular structure of earth and stone that normally covered a megalithic monument
megalith	large stone used in prehistoric monuments
menhir	large stone, often crudely cut and placed vertically in the ground
mesquita	mosque
microlith	small stone
midden	refuse heap
mihrab	a niche in a mosque usually indicating the direction of Mecca
monolith	a single, large stone, as a menhir
mosteiro	monastery
Mozarab	Christian under the Moors (used in reference to architecture)
Mudejar	architecture of Moslems under the Christians
necropolis	burial site
Neolithic	New Stone Age
oppidum	fortified settlement of the Iron Age
orca	a type of collective tomb (see **anta**)
palaestra	gymnasium
paleo	old, early
paleolithic	Old Stone Age
pedra escrita	engraved stone
pelourinho	pillory column of stone
penha	cliff, rock
peristyle	covered passageway around an open patio of a Roman villa

petroglyph	rock engraving or painting
polychrome	of several colours
ponte	bridge
portico	colonnade
povoado	settlement
quinta	country estate or farm
ruinas	ruins
rupestrian	stone
sarcophagus, -i	coffin
serra	mountain range
stele, -ae	a stone slab frequently decorated with inscriptions or carvings
tablinium	reception room or study in a Roman villa
tabularium	archives for official documents
tegulae	tiles
tepidarium	warm room in Roman baths
termas	baths
Terra Sigillata	type of pottery prevalent during the first three centuries of the Roman empire
tesselae	small cubes of stone, glass or ceramics used in the making of mosaics
tholos/tholoi	funerary monument with a false cupola used during the Chalcolithic period consisting of a chamber and corridor covered by a tumulus
triclinium	couch used by Romans for reclining when eating, or room containing one
tumulus	burial mound (see **mamoa**)
vicus	small population constituting a kind of village or hamlet
vivarium	pond for raising fish for eating
zoomorphic	in the shape of an animal

Bibliography

Alarcão, Jorge de. *Portugal Romano.* 4th rev. ed. Vol. 33, Historia Mundi. Lisbon (1987).

———. *Roman Portugal.* Vols. 1 and 2. Warminster (1988).

Albino dos Santos Pereira Lopo. *Apontamentos Arqueológicos.* Braga (1987).

Albuquerque e Castro, L. de and O. da Veiga Ferreira. "As pinturas rupestres da serra dos Louções." *Conímbriga* 2-3 (1960-61): 203-221.

Alves Dias, Manuela, Caetano de Melo Beirão, and Luís Coelho. "Duas Necrópoles da Idade do Ferro do Baixo-Alentejo: Ourique." *Arqueólogo Português,* série iii 4 (1970): 175-219.

Anderson, James M. *Ancient Languages of the Hispanic Peninsula.* Lanham, Md. (1988).

Barker, G. *Prehistoric Farming in Europe.* Cambridge (1985).

Beleza Moreira, José. *Cabeceiras de Sepultura do Museu de Torres Vedras.* Torres Vedras (1982).

Blagg, T.F.C. et al., eds. *Papers in Iberian Archaeology.* BAR International Series, Oxford (1984).

Boardman, John. *The Greeks Overseas: Their Early Colonies and Trade.* London (1980).

Cardoso, João Luís, A. Santinho Cunha, and Delberto de Aguiar. *O Homen Pré-histórico no Concelho de Oeiras.* Estudos de Antropologia Física. Estudos Arqueológicos de Oeiras 2. Oeiras (1991).

Cardozo, Mário. *Citânia de Briteiros e Castro de Sabroso.* Sociedade Martins Sarmento. Guimarães (1990).

Castro Nunes, João de. *Introdução ao Estudo da Cultura Megalítica no Curso Inferior do Alva.* Coimbra (1981).

——— et al. *O Acampamento Militar Romano da Lomba do Canho (Arganil).* Arganil (1988).

Chapman, R.W. *Emerging Complexity: the later prehistory of Southeast Spain, Iberia and the West Mediterranean.* Cambridge (1990).

Childe, V. Gordon. *The Dawn of European Civilization.* 6th rev. ed. London (1957).

Coelho, Luis. "Inscrições da Necrópole Proto-Histórica da Herdade do Pêgo (Ourique)" *Arqueólogo Português* iii 5 (1971): 167-80.

Colóquio Internacional. Arte Pré-Histórica. Almansor. *Revista de Cultura* No. 7. Montemor-o-Novo (1989).

Damião Peres, *Como nasceu Portugal.* Porto (1967).

Da Ponte, Salete. *Sellium. Tomar Romana.* Tomar (1989).

D'Encarnação, José. *Grottes Pré-Historiques de Alapraia, Estoril.* Estoril (1979).

Farinha dos Santos, M. "Novas gravuras rupestres descobertas na Gruta do Escoural." *Rev. Guimarães, 77* (1-2) (1967): 18-34.

_____.*Prehistoria de Portugal*. Lisbon (1985).

Fernando de Almeida, D. *Egitânia. Historia e Arqueologia Lisbon (1956)*.

Ferreira de Almeida, C.A. "O monumento com forno de Sanfins e as escavações de 1973." *Actas III Congresso Nac. de Arq. Porto* (1975): 149-172.

Fragoso de Lima, José. *Monografia Arqueológica do Concelho de Moura. Moura (1988)*.

García Fernández-Albalat, Blanca. *Guerra y Religión en la Gallaecia y la Lusitania Antigua*. A Coruña (1990).

Gil Mantas, Vasco. "Inscrições Romanas do Museu Municipal de Torres Vedras."*Conimbriga 21* (1982): 5-99.

Harden, Donald. *The Phoenicians*. New York (1962).

Harrison, Richard J. *The Bell Beaker Cultures of Spain and Portugal. Cambridge, Mass. (1977)*.

Hauschild, Theodor. "Zur Typologie römischer. Tempel auf der Iberischen Halbinsel." *Homenaje a Saenz de Buruaga*. Badajoz. (1982), 145-56.

_____. A villa romana de Milreu, Estói (Algarve). *Arqueologia,* Oporto 9 (1984): 94-104.

_____. Arte Visigótica. *Historia da Arte em Portugal*. Lisbon (1987).

Historia da Arte em Portugal. Edited by Publicações Alfa. S.A., Lisbon (1986). Sections pertaining to (*a*) Arte Paleolítica (*b*) Arte rupestre pós-glaciária (*c*) Arte Megalítica (*d*) Arte do Bronze Final e da Idade do Ferro (*e*) Arquitectura romana (*f*) Mosaico romano (*g*) Arte Visigótica.

Horta Ferreira, M.A. and T. Bubner. "Novos materiais de Palmela." *Arqueólogo Português,* iii 7-9 (1974-77): 113-124.

Instituto Português do Património Cultural. Dpto. de Arqueologia. *Roteiros da Arqueologia Portuguesa. Lisboa e Arredores*. Lisbon (1986).

_____. *Arqueologia no Vale do Tejo*. Lisbon (1986).

_____.*Roteiros da Arqueologia Portuguesa. Miróbriga*. Lisbon (1990).

Jorge, Vítor de Oliveira, et al. *Nova História de Portugal. Vol I. Portugal - Das Origens a Romanização*. Lisbon (1990).

Kalb, Philine and Martin Höck. Cabeço da Bruxa, Alpiarça (Distrikt Santarém). *Madrider Mitteilungen* 21 (1980): 91-104.

_____. Alto do Castelo, Alpiarça, (Distrikt Santarém). *Madrider Mitteilungen* 23 (1982): 145- 51.

_____. Moron-Historisch und Archäologisch (Tafel 20). *Madrider Mitteilungen* 25 (1984): 92-102.

_____.*Cerâmica de Alpiarça*. Câmara Municipal de Alpiarça, Casa Museu dos Patudos em colaboração com o Instituto Arqueológico Alemão de Lisboa (1985).

_____. *Studien zu den Militärgrenzen Roms III*. Aalen 3 Internationaler Limeskongress (1983): 696-700.

Kayserling, Meyer. *História dos Judeus em Portugal*. Translated from German by Gabriele Borchardt Corrêa da Silva and Anita Novinsky. São Paulo (1971).

Keay, S. J. *Roman Spain*. Berkeley and London (l988).

Kunst, Michael and Leonel Joaquim Trindade. Zur Besiedlungsgeschichte des Sizandrotals (Tafel 3-14). *Madrider Mitteilungen* 31 (1990): 34-82.
_____. *Sternstructen der Archëologie Portugal.* Göttingen (n.d.).
Lemos Regalo, Henrique de. *Levantamento Arqueológico do Concelho de Vila Verde.* Vila Verde (1987).
Lewthwaite, J. "The Transition to Food Production: a Mediterranean Perspective." in *Hunters in Transition*, edited by M. Zvelebil Cambridge (1986).
Lipiner, Elias. *O Tempo dos Judeus segundo as Ordenações do Reino.* São Paulo (1982).
Livermore, H.V. *A New History of Portugal.* Cambridge (1967).
Marco Simón, Francisco. *Las Celtas.* Historia 16. Madrid (1990).
Martins, Manuela. A ocupação do Bronze Final da Citânia de S. Julião, em Vila Verde. *Trabalhos de Antropologia e Etnologia.* Câmara Municipal de Vila Verde (1986):197-222.
_____. *A Citânia de S. Julião, Vila Verde.* Braga. Cadernos de Arqueologia 2 (1988).
_____. *O Castro do Barbudo, Vila Verde.* Braga. Cadernos de Arqueologia 3 (1989).
Mattoso, José. *Identificação de um País.* Ensaio sobre as Origens de Portugal 1096-1325. Vol. 1-Oposição, Vol. 2-Composição. 2nd ed. Lisbon (1986).
Mendes Correia, A. "A Lusitânia Pre-romana" in *Historia de Portugal*, edited by Damião Peres, 77 ff. Lisbon (1928).
Mendes dos Remedios, J. *Os Judeus em Portugal.* Edited by F. França Amado. Coimbra (1895).
Moçárabe em Peregrinação de Mértola ao Cabo de S. Vicente. Lisbon (1990).
Moreira, Alvaro. *Santo Tirso Arqueológico.* Santo Tirso (1991).
Nowell, C. *A History of Portugal.* New York (1952).
Nunes Ribeiro, F. *O Bronze Meridional Português.* Beja (l965). Note: this booklet contains additional bibliography.
_____. *A Villa Romana de Pisões.* Beja (l972).
Oliveira Marques, Antonio Henrique de. *History of Portugal. Vol. I, From Lusitania to Empire.* New York and London (1972).
Paço, A. do. "A necrópole de Alapraia." *Anais Academia Portuguêsa da Historia.* 2nd series, 6 (1955): 28-140.
_____. "'Castro de Vila Nova de S. Pedro. X.' Campanha de escavações de 1956 (20a)." *Anais Academia Portuguêsa da Historia.* 2nd series, 8 (1958): 43-91.
_____ and E. Sangmeister. "'Castro de Vila Nova de S. Pedro. VIII' Campanha de escavação de 1955 (19 a)." *Anais Academia Portuguêsa da Historia.* 2nd series, 7 (1956): 93-144.
Phillips, Patricia. *Early Farmers of West Mediterranean Europe.* London (1975).
_____. *The Prehistory of Europe.* London (1980).
Piggott, Stuart. *Ancient Europe from the Beginnings of Agriculture to Classical Antiquity.* New York (1965).
Pimenta Ferro, Maria José. *Os Judeus em Portugal no Século XIV.* Lisbon (1979).
_____. *Os Judeus em Portugal no Século XV.* Vol. 1. Lisbon (1982).

Princeton Encyclopedia of Classical Sites. Richard Stillwell, ed. Princeton
(1976).

Read, Jan. *The Moors in Spain and Portugal.* London (1974).

Ribeiro, Carlos. *Notícia da Estação Humana de Leceia.* Estudos
Arqueológicos de Oeiras 1 (1991).

Robertson, Ian. *Blue Guide: Portugal.* 3rd ed. London (1989).

Rodríguez Colmenero, Antonio. *Aquae Flaviae. I Fontes Epigráficas.* Chaves
(1987).

Roe, Derek. *Prehistory: an Introduction.* Berkeley and Los Angeles (1970).

Sangmeister, E., H. Schubart and L. Trindade. *Escavações no Castro
Eneolítico do Zambujal (Torres Vedras, Portugal) l964.* Torres Vedras
(1966).

Savory, H. N. *Spain and Portugal: the Prehistory of the Iberian Peninsula.*
London (1968).

Service, Alisair and Jean Bradbery. *A Guide to the Megaliths of Europe.*
Herts (1979).

Stanislawski, D. *The Individuality of Portugal.* Austin (1959).

Straus, L.G. *Iberia Before the Iberians.* Albuquerque (1992).

Teixeira, C and Mendes Corrêa, *A Jazida Prehistórica de Eira Pedrinha.*
Serviços Geológicos de Portugal. Lisbon (1949).

Torres, Cláudio and Luís Alves da Silva. *Mértola, Vila Museu.* 2nd ed.
Mértola (1990).

Trend, J. B. *Portugal.* London (1956).

Untermann, Jürgen. "Lusitanisch, Keltiberisch, Keltisch Studia Palaeo-
hispanica." *Actas del IV Coloquio sobre Lenguas y Culturas
Palaeohispánicas.* Victoria-Gasteiz (1985): 57-76.

Van Doren Stern, Philip. *Prehistoric Europe from Stone Age Man to the
Early Greeks.* New York (1969).

Varela Gomes, Mário and Carlos Tavares da Silva. *Levantamento
Arqueológico do Algarve.* Vila do Bispo (1987).

Veríssimo Serrão, Joaquim. *História de Portugal. Estado, Pátria e Nação
(1080-1415).* 2nd rev. ed. Lisbon (1977).

Whittle, A. *Neolithic Europe: a survey.* Cambridge (1985).

Zbyszewski, G. "Le Quaternaire du Portugal." *Bol. Soc. Geol. de Portugal.* 13
(1-21) (1958):1-227.

_____. "La céramique de la culture du vase campaniforme du Portugal—
Essai de systématisation." *Com. Serv. Geo. de Portugal,* 63 (1978):
449-520.

INDEX OF TOWNS AND VILLAGES